SANDRIN

The Story of a Royal Home

Helen Cathcart

SAPERE
BOOKS

SANDRINGHAM

Published by Sapere Books.

20 Windermere Drive, Leeds, England, LS17 7UZ,
United Kingdom

saperebooks.com

ISBN: 978-1-80055-401-6.

To you, dearest Ma'am, in the hope that this book will give you pleasure.

TABLE OF CONTENTS

1: ALBERT EDWARD'S SURVEY

I

In the raw dawn of Monday, February 3rd 1862, a young man drove across London, bound on an errand that was to change his life and alter the environment and outlook of the monarchy. The awakening streets were still draped here and there with weather-tattered mourning, for it was only seven weeks since the sudden and shocking death of the Prince Consort and the edict of national observance remained in force.

The young man had been at the heart of that Windsor drama, hurrying across England to reach the death chamber in the small hours and keep vigil at the bedside, only to receive no flicker of recognition from the dying man. In the deepest moment of grief, the youth had flung himself into his mother's arms, striving tenderly to comfort her and fervently protesting, "I will be all you wish!" Now his journey was the irretrievable sequel of that promise. A mere boy of twenty, stocky, pink-complexioned, Albert Edward, Prince of Wales, was pitched drastically towards his future.

The young Prince was not alone. He scarcely knew what it was to be alone. His two companions in the dark brougham, frock-coated and top-hatted, were General Bruce, his dour and watchful governor, and Major Teesdale, the Prince's equerry, cold and ramrod-stiff. Winner of the Victoria Cross for valour in the Crimea, the Major had been sternly briefed by the Prince Consort three years earlier to instruct the heir to the Throne in avoiding "the frivolity and foolish vanity of dandyism" and to prevent "lounging ways" and "slouching gait". The General's still stricter mandate was from the Queen, "to regulate all the Prince's movements" and instil his ward at all times with "the conscientious discharge of his duties towards God and man". Borne along by this gloomy and frustrated couple, imprisoned, penitent, packaged and conveyed in the clothing of mourning, blindly engaged to his dead father's wishes, the Prince of Wales was as helplessly bound by self-reproach that February day as if pinioned in a straitjacket.

At Shoreditch Station the black-clad trio were solemnly joined by Sir Charles Phipps, Keeper of the Privy Purse, and the circumspect and reticent Mr. White, the Crown solicitor. Thus there were four sombre elderly figures to shepherd the Prince on his first visit of inspection to Sandringham, ushering him through the outward show of independence in a decision already firmly agreed — and practically settled — between the Queen and her Prime Minister.

Perhaps it was the circumstances of bereavement surrounding the purchase that later made Queen Victoria consider Sandringham an unlucky house. She visited it with striking rarity: only twice in forty years and only once without the imperative summons of dangerous illness.[1] Possibly the Queen harboured a lingering resentment, scarcely expressed even to herself, that her husband, her "beloved angel", had after all been deceived and outwitted in the deal and that she had herself been cruelly swindled. But both superstition and unconcealed animosity would have deepened if she could have foreseen the grim record of the next hundred years.

For kings have undoubtedly caught their death of cold at Sandringham. Princes have grappled with typhoid in its

---

[1] The Queen went back and forth between Sandringham and Windsor during the Prince of Wales' illness in December 1871, but this is usually regarded as one visit.

bedrooms and an heir presumptive to the British throne perished there miserably of pneumonia. An Empress of Russia praised the "marine air" but found less to admire in the lumbago brought on by Sandringham dampness; while her sister, the beautiful and beloved Queen Alexandra, was permanently crippled at Sandringham by an attack of rheumatic fever. Disraeli wisely shunned the place in fair April "snowing and sleeting with a due East wind" and even the architect was worried into a premature grave, his lease of life expiring most inappropriately, poor man, on Christmas Eve.

Yet Albert Edward, after he became King Edward VII, was to dub Sandringham "the house I like best" and his sons and grandsons were to accord it an affection among royal homes far surpassing their regard for any other. "Dear old Sandringham", said King George V, "the place I love better than anywhere else in the world" and King George VI was to echo "I have always been so happy here…"

The Duke of Windsor, fourteen years after abdicating the throne, was wistfully to recall the merry Sandringham Christmas of his boyhood, "Dickens in a Cartier setting… the whole family reunited, the whole estate wearing a festive air". So the chicanery and secrecy and mournful frustration of the purchase were to lead out at last to sunnier channels of human happiness, in the sequence of domestic events that we may hope to trace in this chronicle.

In 1862, however, Sandringham lay at the end of the line, and seven miles beyond. A neighbouring landowner, Lord Suffield, saw the shabby, run-down estate as no more than a "wind-swept, barren, sandy moorland" and a local parson was soon to describe it as "the wildest and most out-of-the-way place imaginable". Yet the very solitude and isolation were compulsive inducements in the purchase, coupled as they were with the timely high-pressure salesmanship of the most persuasive man in England.

Wary and irresolute, the Prince Consort had agreed that its position, in the north-west hinterland of Norfolk, so far removed from the temptations of town life, was a prime asset. "And *no human power* will make me swerve from *what he* decided and wished," the Queen had written in that now familiar letter of anguish after ten days of widowhood. "I apply this particularly as regards our children — Bertie, etc. — for whose future he had traced everything so carefully."

In 1862, then, Sandringham lay obscure and unremarked at the nape of Norfolk, where the eastern counties of England seem eager to break from the mainland and thrust energetically towards the North Sea. From the London terminus of Shoreditch Station the Great Eastern Railway ran nearly due north for ninety-eight miles, through studious Cambridge and ecclesiastical Ely, through the flat vistas of farmland and fen, but then came the desolate world's end of metropolitan man.

Beyond the gaunt and neglected warehouses of depressed Lynn — with six hundred empty tenements in those days — only the rough embankments of a new and unfinished railway straggled across the pastures and marshes towards Hunstanton, a searing trail of cranes and giant tripods and confused carts and heaps of carstone rubble, embedded in squelching mud. The age of steam had scarcely touched the ancient villages at this remote north-west fringe of Norfolk. This development still lay in the future, an unturned key, enigmatic as the royal future of Sandringham itself.

II

Though so young, the Prince enjoyed one unnoticed advantage on that February journey: Albert Edward was already in fact not unacquainted with the theory and practice of architecture. He had lived from his earliest years within sound of the mason's mallet and chisel, and his father's building projects had followed one on another with ever-increasing momentum: the Prince of Wales could scarcely remember a time when architectural plans or sketches had not found a place on the Prince Consort's tidy desk or when life with father had not included a stroll to see how the newest wing, the latest structure, was progressing.

First there had been the building of Osborne, filling the background of infancy with memories of miasmic dust and confusion. From his sixth to his tenth year, the construction of the two eastern wings saw his boyhood never quite freed from the allurements of scaffolding; the exciting ascents while grasping his father's hand; the transforming magic of solid walls, rooms and whole palaces rising foot by foot from the ground. He had explored, on rare occasions when he could escape from his tutor, a friendly, mysterious and garish world of bricklayers and carpenters. He had sometimes been permitted to clamber to dizzy platforms where his father gravely held consultations with architects and surveyors while the Prince experimentally stubbed his toe in wet mortar.

When Prince Albert Edward was twelve years old, there came the marvel of the Swiss Cottage, which was brought in sections from its native land and erected in the grounds of Osborne as a playhouse where the Prince and his brothers could actually learn the firm accomplishments of carpentry and bricklaying. That year of 1853 also saw the intense family preoccupation with the new Balmoral Castle, with sketches of towers and turrets and gables and elevations, with discussions on fireplaces and wallpapers until — when he was a boy of fourteen — Albert Edward could walk with his mother through the completed building, the accomplished and tangible dream. And for all the severe and unremitting regime under his tutors, the Prince could affectionately share his mother's joy, "the house... charming, the rooms delightful, the furniture, papers, everything — perfection".

Meanwhile Buckingham Palace, too, underwent a continuous turmoil of renovation and addition. Here again scaffolding and sand and builders' stores seemed an eternal part of the unchanging scene. The building of Blore's east front was in progress from the time Prince Edward was eight until he was ten years of age. The removal of the Marble Arch stone by stone from the Palace forecourt to Marble Arch capped his tenth year with triumphant proof that with men and horses and the Office of Works all things were possible.

The young Prince knew of rooms in the Palace where enticing architectural models were to be seen, and perhaps timidly played with. Eager that his son should be encouraged in an understanding of the fine arts, the Prince Consort would not have forgone the opportunity of giving instruction in classic tradition and design, in perspective and proportion and draughtsmanship.

The first wave of paternal planning and construction culminated in the Great Exhibition of 1851. On the opening day the young Prince, in Highland costume, played no inconspicuous role, and there had been visits innumerable while the building of the Crystal Palace was in progress. The boy watched with delight one day when three hundred workmen jumped up and down in one of the galleries to demonstrate its strength.

Then followed the rebuilding of the whole south-west wing and the kitchens of Buckingham Palace. Pennethorne's ballroom was ready in 1856, when the fifteen-year-old Prince of Wales was allowed to stay up late for the Crimean victory ball. In brief, Albert Edward had reason to regard architects and designers and decorators as essential a part of the royal adult world as statesmen and visiting German relatives.

Sir Charles Eastlake, then the president of the Royal Academy, was preoccupied with interior design and "household taste"; a celebrity high in royal favour with whom the young Prince could share some of the "refined and agreeable conversation" which favourably impressed his elders. The Prince was conversant with Pugin and Gilbert Scott, if not the principles of the Gothic revival. And Albert Edward was to prove that he had been capably brought up with the hollow-brick construction, the heated linen cupboards, dust shafts and well-ventilated larders of his father's "model dwellings for the working classes".

Ruskin had advised that the Prince of Wales should be encouraged to think for himself, particularly if he were taught that "one of the main duties of Princes was to provide for the preservation of perishing frescoes…" At seventeen, when the Prince was permitted to spend three months in Rome, his tutors equipped him with an overwhelming schedule of studies that nevertheless enabled him to inspect "ancient and modern works of art and ancient monuments" nearly every afternoon.

There, as Sir Sidney Lee says "he collected much miscellaneous knowledge of the buildings, monuments and artistic treasures of the city", as well as meeting the Duke of St. Albans, whom Lee describes as "a young man of weak character". But the Duke's youthful and impassioned fervour for architecture coloured the Prince's mind, as we shall see, and its imprint remains on Sandringham to this day.

Albert Edward's own bent was to be more clearly in evidence two years later when he embarked on the great adventure of a royal journey to North America. His letters home, though bald and dutiful, demonstrated an architectural attentiveness. In Newfoundland he noted St. John's as "a very picturesque seaport town." In Washington the Prince was stirred almost to eloquence, "The President's house is a very nice one, and the rooms are really very fine, and comfortably furnished. Washington is a fine looking town and contains some striking buildings. The finest is the Capitol... I shall bring home some drawings which will give you a much better idea of it... we might easily take some hints for our own buildings which are so very bad". Of Mount Vernon he reported with less enthusiasm, "The house itself is unfortunately in very bad repair, and is rapidly falling into decay". Obviously the Prince returned home with a new eye, to complete the plans of his formal education, first at Oxford and then Cambridge.

He found his father poring over new plans for the "improvement" of Whippingham Church, a homely Saxon structure near Osborne on the northern flanks of the Isle of Wight, which the Prince Consort was now to turn into a pinnacled and Germanic edifice that might have come in its entirety direct from Coburg or the Black Forest. Then there were new dwellings at Windsor and Papa's model dairy at Frogmore, with its quattrocento tiles and ceramic decorations.

The Prince Consort, unlike his Wittelsbach cousins, was not too deeply touched by building mania although his experiments with style ranged eagerly from the medieval to the Italianate and "high fashion" design of his own day, and his interest was close and never-ending.

Even the year of his death, when he was fretful and unwell, saw him supervising the plans for his mother-in-law's Ionic mausoleum at Frogmore, a task eased by his architect, Mr.

Albert Jenkins Humbert, who had co-operated admirably in planning Whippingham Church and seemed always so likeable, helpful and sympathetic.

These essays in brick and stone, in "taste and art", all formed the constant undercurrent of family interest during Albert Edward's visits home from university. The incessant exchanges with Mr. Turnbull, of the Board of Works; the renovations and alterations which James Pennethorne was executing at Marlborough House — shortly to become the Prince of Wales' London home — and the building of a little museum for the children at Osborne, were all recurrent topics in conversation.

The Prince of Wales was primarily studying law and history at Cambridge but we are told that he also "saw much of Professor Robert Willis, an authority on architecture". He saw even more of the young Duke of St. Albans, now a fellow undergraduate, and the two were boon companions. Wealthy and unfettered, St. Albans was devoted to architecture with such impressive ardour that he was already commissioning a Gothic mansion of his own and he waxed lyrical with praise of the "vigour" and "go" of Samuel Teulon, an architect who had carried out one of the largest houses in England at Tortworth, Lord Ducie's place in Gloucestershire, which had a hundred bedrooms. But this was to be excelled by the country house which Teulon was shortly to undertake for St. Albans himself at Bestwood, in Nottinghamshire, destined to be the greatest Gothic private house ever built.

In the undergraduate discussions, the Prince no doubt loyally advanced the claims of Pennethorne or Barry or Albert Jenkins Humbert only to be swept aside by the excitement of Samuel Sanders Teulon, his fierce and martial churches, his polychromatic efforts, his bold experiments.

The enthusiasm was infectious. It is certain that the Prince of Wales was impressed as St. Albans spread out the preliminary drawings of Bestwood Lodge and the effect was to be far-reaching. The Prince was a good listener and though he may not have followed his friend's higher flights into Middle Pointed Gothic, the ducal rhapsodies fell on to fertile soil.

During his last term at Cambridge, in the autumn of 1861, the Prince greeted with some excitement the prospect that he was also to have a country place of his own. His parents, however, accorded him no freedom of choice and deemed it unwise to trust him with any detail of the plans they were hatching at no small expense.

III

Albert Edward's first visit of inspection to Sandringham occurred, in fact, on an auspiciously dry and cheerful February day. Although his four companions were so staid, even morose, and elderly, spirits no doubt rose as they stepped into a brushed and polished first class railway carriage at Shoreditch and the train gathered speed through the London suburbs towards an exhilarating twenty-five miles per hour.

With mischievous presence of mind, indeed, the Prince had quietly invited a Cambridge crony, one Tommy Bagge, who lived in King's Lynn, to meet the train there. He was thus one up in gamesmanship as the soft Hertfordshire farmlands gave place to the flat and featureless landscape of the Fens, and the news of his coming ahead by electric telegraph.

The train drew into Lynn at 12.20, only five minutes behind time. Word had spread from lip to lip, a crowd had gathered, and two carriages were waiting, one supplied to order by the landlord of the Globe, the other furnished by the mayor, determined that his carriage alone should be honoured by the royal posterior.

The cheerful face of Tommy Bagge smiled in welcome. Mr. White, the Crown solicitor, presented Mr. Janson, the vendor's solicitor, who in turn presented Mr. Beck, the agent or factor of the Sandringham estate. The mayor pressed forward and mine host of the Globe perhaps played his last forlorn hand by suggesting that the two pairs of horses might be teamed together. But this the Prince declined, according to a contemporary eyewitness of the scene, "by reason of the attention the equipage would involve".

The Globe was nevertheless to provide luncheon at the house; a cook and waiters and hampers had been sent ahead, and the innkeeper could suitably follow in his cab. We may suppose that the agent and the equerry led the way with the legal gentlemen in their own conveyance, the Prince following with Bagge and the Court officials. Such was the first royal cavalcade to Sandringham, the vanguard of emperors and premiers, potentates and statesmen, the procession of illustrious trippers of at least a hundred years.

The crayons of research sketch the scene from the old accounts … the hats of the onlookers doffed as the carriages wheeled from the station, the travellers' coat-collars turned up as they left the shelter of the streets and faced the bleak wind across the flat water meadows on the Gaywood road.

Chatting eagerly to Bagge, Albert Edward would have glanced out at the waterworks beyond the leafless trees and presently Bagge would have pointed out the mansion of his own family home, where his father was lord of the manor. Northwards through the villages of Wootton and Castle Rising, we can still catch the creak of the carriages, the jingle of harness, the smart clop of hooves.

Bagge may have been prompted by local pride to point out that the mound of Castle Rising was probably older than Windsor itself. Fresh from his history studies, the Prince knew that Edward III — son of that Edward II who had been the first of the English crown princes to bear the title of Prince of Wales — had bought the castle for his mother, Queen Isabella, and that his son in turn, the Black Prince, had once held possession within the now-ruined walls.

Five hundred years of ancestral history were joined in a glint of time as the carriages rattled past and Victoria's heir gazed out, with a lively and not untrained eye, at the stones of the Norman keep.

And now the sea marshes to the left and west were wilder, ebbing into wintry mists, while to the right and east the heaths and farmsteads grew more unkempt and solitary. Hereabouts the Prince perhaps caught the first glimpse of his future home, a blue-grey rooftop with a dozen chimneystacks, lodged on a rising bluff of woods and moorland two miles distant to the north.

The meandering and sluggish Babingley River was crossed and Tommy Bagge, at the Prince's side, had sufficient local knowledge to indicate that his royal friend's new domain was beginning. Away to the left the gables of old Babingley manor house proclaimed part of the Sandringham property. But the little procession presently veered to the right. The wheels grated on a rougher road inclining across the heathery moor. A thatched and silent lodge was passed, tawny lengths of old park walling, a view of twisted oaks, a neglected avenue of lime and fir.

The scene is all changed now and yet the child of Balmoral may have enjoyed a sensation of coming home, for it was as if a little bit of Scotland, with pine and heather, had been dropped on the uplands above the marshes, and some hint of Osborne gleamed in the pale frontage of the house.

Craning expectantly, Albert Edward would first have seen the staring façade of Sandringham Hall through the trees, fronting a reedy lake, before his carriage swung around the northern flank, to pass through a rusting iron gateway towards the arched and buttressed, scrolled and chequered, multi-coloured entrance porch, half Romanesque, half Gothic, at the rear.

IV

The house that Albert Edward saw, the house successfully foisted upon his father, was a long three-storied mid-Georgian mansion, clothed in shabby painted stucco. It gave the first impression of a long and graceful façade, of a balanced and elegant line of sash windows, twelve or more, each with its dozen small panes of glimmering glass, but this superficial first glimpse was illusive. It was an ungainly house, a robust slate-roofed block or rather a huddle of blocks, as if a giant had rammed two oblong boxes of uneven length side by side, and roofed them separately, filling out the nooks and corners of these parallel but unequal ranges with four prim cubes, each with separate roof and chimney.

The pleasant proportions of the two lower floors might have sufficed, but an intoxicated architect had severed them with string courses and surmounted them with a third attic storey and capped this equally with broad gables like wigwams which stood encamped, thanks to later alterations, in a coppice of mock Elizabethan chimneys.

Albert Edward, we may suppose, took in little of this at first glance. It was left to the Duke of St. Albans, paying remote future visits as a guest, to argue which came first, the long garden frontage or the shorter entrance front, a riddle as impossible to solve as the enigma of the chicken and the egg. The garden block had perhaps thrust two short two-storied wings eastward to form three sides of a square or perhaps they had come later and the entrance block and garden front had first lived in harmony.

Untroubled by these speculations, the Prince of Wales no doubt paused to look up appreciatively before entering his future home, as house-buyers will do the world over. And instantly there was that variegated, richly ornamented entrance porch, two floors high, creamy stone and white brick and red, unashamedly challenging the old-fashioned white house.

To our plainer taste this fussy pedimented lobby would have seemed a discoloured sore thumb, imposed on the resentful old building. It could at best be reminiscent only of the Victorian charms of, say, the old Kensington town hall, or a municipal library. Yet to young and rebellious Albert Edward it appeared enriching and desirable, an embellishment such as St. Albans had constantly praised, full of vigour and go. He must have learned with intense joy that it was by none other than Samuel Sanders Teulon.

The sheer coincidence glowed with welcome and caused the Prince, apt to be influenced by such trivia, to bask in its warmth. Decorated with floral panels, the interior rooms were not without colour, and it was a point of the sale that the former owner was leaving his furniture.

As he explored the rooms, especially the reception suite on the western garden side, Albert Edward would have found them "fine" and "commodious". He would have been assured that fireplaces and floors were "solid" and "substantial", for such adjectives were much in vogue.

From the higher bedrooms, on a clear day, one could look across the Wolferton marshes and the Wash all the way to Boston Stump, though probably the Prince was not told that a clear view of the Boston steeple invariably heralded rain.

Over the Globe's luncheon Mr. Beck was no doubt encouraged to praise the sport and kindred enjoyments that the estate afforded. The Prince was reassuringly informed of his tenants and assuredly not warned of the expenditure needed for their damp and decaying hovels. He was probably told of the sheep-farming prospects on the chalk uplands east of Sandringham towards Houghton Hall and perhaps Mr. Janson talked expansively of the affairs of the Walpoles, who had occupied Houghton a hundred years, or else cited the enterprising example of neighbouring Holkham, where the young Earl of Leicester was profitably reclaiming land from the sea.

In the dining-room a bay window had been recently thrust out to command a view of the lake, and a low wall of openwork chain-pattern brick divided the gravelled terrace from the rough slopes of lawn. This balustrade was also a Teulon refurbishment, as were the soaring mock Elizabethan chimneys that crowned the roof, yet better still was to come. Janson and Beck could play their trump card. For immediately adjoining the house to the south was a glass conservatory with a gabled end wall built in a vari-coloured pattern of carstone and brick. With its triple arched windows, its stained glass, is corrugated pediments and bulbous finials, the style was perhaps more suited to a chapel than a hothouse. But this also was the work of the admired Teulon and Albert Edward regarded it with lasting esteem.

Every other stick and stone of Sandringham Hall was to be swept away with the changes of time. The conservatory was to yield to a billiard room. Yet Teuton's curious polychromatic wall remains, his rebuilt chimneys still dominate the Sandringham roofline and the elements of his porch can still be seen.

Spurred by such attractions, the Prince was in a happy frame of mind after lunch when he set out to inspect the estate. He clearly expected to see everything in the course of the afternoon, or as much as time allowed. Two of "his" tenant farmers, Mr. Joshua Freeman and Mr. Bradfield, paid their respects, and it would have been strange if Albert Edward had not felt the surging pride of new ownership.

He strode through barnyards deep in February mud; he beamed with an innocent and approving eye on cattle, pigs and poultry, possibly unaware that the stock belonged to the tenants.

Watching him leap in and out of the carriage to inspect fields and plantations, farms and hamlets, the solicitors were no doubt glad to wait, drawing breath, while the Prince and Tommy Bagge explored. The estate spread through the six parishes of Sandringham, Babingley, Wolferton, Appleton, West Newton and Dersingham, and the Prince energetically toured it — and sealed his future — within two hours.

The royal party punctually caught the 4.40 evening train back to London, but not before the enterprising Lynn reporters had thrust their questions and the Prince had satisfied local pride by expressing his contentment and the hope that Sandringham would become his shortly.

The legal gentlemen in fact could safely gross up their fees — manna from Heaven to Mr. Janson — and rest assured that "completion" would not long be delayed. Had the weather changed, a cloud of doubt might have arisen, just as rain had made the Queen decide some twenty years earlier not to buy a residence in the Western Highlands. But the Prince was elated to snatch a feather from the extravagant cap of the Duke of St. Albans in the unexpected bonus of Teuton in acquiescing to his dead father's wish.

Next day he hurried to Osborne to assure his mother of his pleasure. What picture he painted of Sandringham, what his rosy illusions were, we may never know. Yet we have the blunt account of a farmer who took up a Sandringham tenancy at about this time to be greeted by "a scene of dirt, ruin and desolation".

We are told of ramshackle houses where bugs swarmed in clusters and rats frisked about, of "model tenants who never asked for repairs and objected to anything that had tumbled down being built up again…" of "roads that had not been mended for years, sinking down in the middle and high at the sides … a sea of mud and slush which increased as the rain set in" and impassable back roads "full of treacherous holes and overgrown with grass". The "utterly exhausted land appeared to have been neither manured nor weeded for years". There were "broken gates and miles of rotten fencing…"

For this nightmare demesne, with the Hall and its furniture, five farms, some inconsiderable lodges and decrepit cottages, a total of 7,000 acres with a potential but improbable rent-roll of £7,000, the Prince of Wales paid £220,000. This was six times more, £188,000 more, than the £35,000 which the Queen had paid for the Balmoral estate, with its 17,400 acres, only ten years before.

It soared seven times higher than the asking price of £30,000 for Osborne which had been considered exorbitant in 1845, and almost equalled indeed the total sum ultimately lavished on Osborne not only for purchase but also for complete rebuilding and furnishing.

In Norfolk itself local tongues notably wagged with inside knowledge. The Prince of Wales' £220,000 was freely compared with the £76,000 paid at the Auction Mart in London when the Sandringham estate, very little altered, had been last on the market twenty-six years earlier.

Those of simple heart may have envied the Prince for having so much to spend, while the worldly marvelled at the two hundred per cent profit that had fallen to — of all people — a middle-aged widower who was officially Lord Palmerston's stepson and may have had a closer natural relationship.

V

The purchase of Sandringham Hall by the Prince of Wales was made public on February 22nd, less than three weeks after his inspection, and the Prince had by that time embarked on a tour to the Holy Land, in posthumous fulfilment of another of his father's plans. Although it need not have been divulged, the private matter of the purchase price was also announced, with a touch of curious royal defiance. More timidly, however, the estimated gross income of £7,000 was not made known, a manoeuvre which prevented anyone from totting up that at twenty years' purchase a capital expenditure of £140,000 would have represented a sum more in line with prudent and realistic economy.

If the outlay of nearly a quarter-million pounds seemed immense — especially so since the Hall was cautiously described as "a shooting box" — criticism of the Queen or her court was unthinkable in her bereavement.

Eighteen years earlier, when ministers and secretaries had advised the Prince Consort against the purchase of Osborne, he had pointed out that the Queen had saved £70,000 of personal income since she came to the throne.

Now, similarly, the annual lands revenue of the Duchy of Cornwall, the hereditary perquisite of the heir-apparent, had accumulated since Albert Edward's birth to a capital sum of some £660,000. If the Prince of Wales elected to squander a third of his fortune on a country estate, the extravagance was not unfitting for a separate private establishment now that he assumed the mantle of "the first gentleman of the land". So shoulders were shrugged with indifference.

Besides, the primary choice had been that of the Prince Consort before his death passed the leading strings to the Queen. "She has had many conversations with her beloved angel and she feels that *she* knows exactly what he wished," Queen Victoria wrote to General Bruce on January 5th. "This being the case the Queen must decide what she thinks the best... She is ready to take the responsibility of this decision upon herself as she feels *sure* she is acting as he would wish."

But the Prince Consort had supervised and husbanded the income of the Duchy estates for twenty years with such diligence that the annual revenue rose from £16,000 in 1841 to nearly £60,000 in the year when his son came of age. Few dared to ask, or troubled to think, why he should be so abruptly lax and prodigal with the resources he had previously harboured with such wisdom.

The royal parents had early recognised the customary right of the Prince of Wales to a domicile of his own and Marlborough House was appropriated to him in 1850 by Act of Parliament, although it was occupied during his minority by the Government School of Design and a museum, the nucleus of the South Kensington arts collection.

The celebration of the Prince's eighteenth birthday may be set as the turning point of parental approval of his equal right to an estate of his own. Thenceforth, the house-hunt was on, though at a tepid and unhurried pace. Newstead Abbey was at one time proposed and Lord Macclesfield offered his estate of Eynsham in Oxfordshire. It is said that the great Norfolk houses of Blickling, Houghton, Holkham and Gunton were considered, but Lord Suffield, the squire of Gunton who became the Prince's equerry, later wrote that Gunton was not for sale. And not for sale, certainly, was Sandringham Hall, for, off the open market, what owner ever foolishly professed to be willing to sell when faced with an eager and persistent buyer?

Before purchasing Osborne, the Queen had consulted her Prime Minister of the day, Sir Robert Peel. Similarly it is evident that Lord Palmerston was approached as Prime Minister for his opinion on the new and looming problem of a country home for the Prince of Wales.

He must have masked his thoughts behind a smile as bland and false as the russet colour of his hair. He could intimate that he knew the very spot, his stepson's place in Norfolk, offering the finest shooting in all England. But it required the merest hint and the faintest shrug of regret: his young stepson, George Spencer Cowper, would have been represented as far too happily absorbed, far too contented in his country estates to be willing to part with them, even to the Prince of Wales.

In reality, the very reverse was the truth. Spencer Cowper spent much of his time in Paris and returned to the mournful atmosphere of Sandringham only under duress. The open acres, the echoing rooms, the reluctant rents, meant little more than one form of security, and whispers persisted a century later that the estate was heavily mortgaged.

When Palmerston as a bachelor of fifty-five married Emily Cowper, a widow of fifty, he had married into her family of five grown children — some were said to be his — and he found Spencer, the youngest son, not the least of his problems.

He had, however, promptly procured him a post with the Foreign Office and became greatly attached to him if only as one of the most wilful and fate-buffeted of all Emily's brood.

Spencer, as we shall see, had a flair for winning the friendship of elderly men, let alone the benevolence of such a close and fatherly mentor. To Palmerston, in his mid-seventies, the thought of reconstituting the boy's fortunes was highly inviting but the glittering prospect of doing so at royal expense offered a triumph second to none.

Palmerston was far too astute and practised not to bide his time. "An able politician ... an indefatigable man of business ... but a man of expediency ... no very high standard of honour and not a grain of moral feeling," the Prince Consort once summed him up in a "private and confidential" letter to a third party.

Palmerston had endured fifteen years of many worse taunts and insults. As Foreign Secretary he clashed repeatedly with the Queen's attitude in foreign affairs. He never minced matters in describing the Queen's foreign relatives: snubs, rebukes, objections and humiliations were exchanged. "The man who embittered our whole life," the Prince Consort described him, in one of the continual diatribes, and Lord John Russell complained of "patience drained to the last jot" in the years of "most harassing warfare ... as umpire between Windsor and Broadlands", Palmerston's home. Though in favour at Windsor, Lord Clarendon could write of the royal pair, "I think they are unfair about Palmerston, and are always ready to let their old rancour against him boil up and boil over."

It would have been surprising if the subject of this relentless feuding had not seen in Sandringham a piquant fee of retribution. In 1859 the battle flared into sharp new conflict as the Prince Consort accused Palmerston of writing pamphlets against him and the Queen acidly returned a letter to her Prime Minister as lacking "the respect which is due from a Minister to his sovereign". But suddenly all was still on the battlefield. One could have heard a pin drop after Prince Albert Edward's coming-of-age, his eighteenth birthday, when the desultory house-hunting first began.

Palmerston played his line with patience and infinite skill. A year later he seemed no nearer his objective when suddenly, in December 1860, *The Times* announced that Mrs. Spencer Cowper had died in Paris. The report was false, but was it in fact inspired by Palmerston? Was it, indeed, a "plant"? The rumour at all events enabled him once more to proffer Sandringham, in the most deft and tactful manner imaginable, and then once again to withdraw it.

There were, of course, risks in the game. Considerable tension was introduced early in 1861 when Charles Kingsley, Albert Edward's Cambridge tutor, recommended the great house of Bramshill in his own parish in Hampshire, so conveniently near Windsor. Palmerston contrived to decry its Jacobean splendours and the idea was dropped. Yet the Prince Consort's mistrust had still to be gently allayed, one cautious step at a time. As late as July 1861, the Prince Consort could still complain of Palmerston's "offensive flattery", and the very challenge was one the old statesman found stimulating.

His friends were struck by his rejuvenation, "For the last twenty years you have not seen Palmerston look as he does now," wrote Earl Cowley. "The warmer breezes have agreed with him wonderfully, the sea has washed all the dye out of his whiskers and given him a bright colour of his own, he has a new set of teeth, and altogether he looks, and I am sure he feels, as if he did not care one straw for any man…"

With growing confidence Palmerston watched the stage being set precisely as he wished it through the autumn. Fate in the guise of Albert Edward's first frolics was playing directly into his hand. The crucial moment came as Albert Edward's twentieth birthday approached. Palmerston, and his lady, were now sufficiently in the royal good books to be invited to Windsor for three days. The Queen and her husband were worried by vague whispers that "Bertie" was being "introduced to dissipations that were new to him". Now was the time to advance the healthy open-air diversions and the trouble-free seclusion of Sandringham and give the news that Spencer might after all be persuaded to part with his paradise. The royal couple were receptive, the line baited, and Palmerston brimming with guile.

"Palmerston was here, three days," wrote Lady Augusta Stanley, the Queen's lady-in-waiting, "and charming he was, younger than ever, and full of jokes. Oh! The jauntiness of him!"

Oh, the jauntiness, indeed, for he had pulled it off. The bait was swallowed, the Prince Consort's irresolution all but conquered, the handshakes exchanged. There remained only the slips at the eleventh hour that might imperil any transaction and Palmerston decided to deliver the final blow. He had only to ensure that the Prince Consort heard the story of Bertie that was rife in every London club. Within a week the tale-bearing was deviously effected and the Prince Consort was told the shocking news that, according to Queen Victoria, "broke my Angel's heart". It concerned an escapade with a woman on Albert Edward's part and the natural consequences that might be anticipated from his youthful recklessness.

The girl was Nellie Clifden, a young actress whom he had met during the summer in Ireland and the talk of a possible child seems to have been mere embroidery. But the Queen and her husband were beside themselves with horror. Suppressing none of his anxiety, the Prince Consort wrote to his son assuring him that all the people round him would do everything to help him and five days later he hurried down to Cambridge to learn in deep and searching conversation that the liaison was at an end. He stayed overnight with Bertie at his lodgings, and returned to London "much relieved", according to the Queen, though feeling out of sorts.

The Prince Consort's feverish anxiety to isolate his heir out of harm's way in the depths of the country was, however, now so overwhelming that Palmerston evidently felt able to name his own price. Then, at this crucial moment, the Prince Consort fell disastrously ill and the whole Sandringham operation was in jeopardy. Now it was Palmerston's turn to be acutely stricken with anxiety as the better part of a quarter of a million pounds threatened to elude his grasp.

As Palmerston's modern biographer, Herbert Bell, has said, he showed alarm when none was felt by the royal physicians. He bustled around the doctors, insisting on fresh consultants, and "no one could have shown more alarm and distress than when the great tragedy of Victoria's life occurred. The Prince's death seems simply to have staggered him". Clarendon, too, remarked that Palmerston was "more shocked and *overwhelmed*" than seemed possible.

Palmerston was, in fact, beside himself. In justice some of his distraught emotion was untarnished by his mercenary hopes for Spencer Cowper. Every man of sensibility was moved by the Queen's bereavement. Yet success in the Sandringham negotiations had been so near completion, so near and now so far. Mr. White, the Crown solicitor, had gone down to Norfolk to confer with his opposite number, but already there were many new voices to caution the Queen and perhaps disrupt the bargain.

Planning his next move, Palmerston was at first unaware that every suggestion of changing the Prince Consort's plans provoked the Queen to near-hysteria. "*No human power* will make me swerve from *what he* decided and wished," she passionately wrote to Uncle Leopold the day after the funeral. "*No one* person, may he be ever so good, ever so devoted, among my servants — is to lead or guide or dictate *to me*." But on what urgent topic did the Queen need dissuasion so soon, except Sandringham?

Palmerston retrieved his composure, picked up the pieces of the nearly shattered transaction and presented himself at Osborne on January 27th. He was a figure of distress, stammering condolences, he brought the conversation dexterously round to Bertie and the Queen was startled that Lord Palmerston should "enter so entirely" into her "anxieties".

Cautiously the Prime Minister skirted the Clifden catastrophe … "*everything was quiet*, he thought there would be no trouble, but *the* difficulty of the moment was Bertie". Such are the Queen's own words. Insidiously, with craftiness mingled with compassion, Palmerston led the sorrowing widow down the garden path This was the day when Lady Augusta Stanley recorded that Palmerston "wept bitterly". And precisely a week later young Bertie hastened to Sandringham on his first visit of inspection.

2: PREDECESSORS IN TITLE

The stones of ten centuries, with perhaps a Roman tile or two from Appleton, lie in the packed rubble of the Sandringham foundations. In the time of Edward the Confessor the land was held by a freeman named Tost under Harold, brother-in-law of the King, but with the Norman Conquest Tost made his farewell to be supplanted by a Norman knight, Robert Fitz-Corbun, who was lord of the manor in 1086 when the Domesday Book somewhat wryly recorded the benefits of occupation.

In Tost's time "and afterwards, one plough-team, now none; then and afterwards five bordars, now none; then and afterwards three servi, now one. And there were 3½ acres of water-meadow. Then and afterwards one plough-team amongst the tenants; then and afterwards one salt-work. Always valued at 20s.". Evidently the bordars or serfs, holding their huts at the lord's pleasure, knew how to make themselves scarce and their reduced circumstances were recorded with one eye on the tax collector. The name was then Sant-Dersingham, the hamlet of the sand-meadow, and the domain was then minor to the manors of Dersingham, Appleton, Babingley and others today ranked within the royal acres.

While Robert Fitz-Corbun was ardently engaged elsewhere in founding his Curzon dynasty, another Norman knight, Peter de Valoins, was busily augmenting his two hundred acres in Dersingham, acquiring land in every direction.

Lord of at least six carthorses and two cows, two teams of oxen, a flock of sheep, a mill, a salt-work and a fishery, he seized twelve acres belonging to a freeman, value twelve pence, and got away with this takeover so successfully that he then grabbed the lands of another twenty-one freemen and appears to have gained official grant of them from the Conqueror.

A century later, however, the Fitz-Corbuns were still securely in possession of Sandringham itself, and from them the estate passed to Simon de Whatefield and then to Reginald de Wode and Alice his wife, who litigated themselves into documented history in 1265 when Reginald impleaded several persons for carrying away his goods.

At Babingley, too, in that year, Robert de Tateshall impleaded a trespasser who had cut down and sold his woods while he, Robert, was held a prisoner of Simon de Montfort, which indicates what could happen while landlords were away at the wars. Shortly afterwards the Abbot of the marshland abbey of St. Benet-at-Holme had an interest here but in 1296 Sir Richard de la Rokele was licensed by King Edward I to exchange his manor in Stoke Holy Cross for that of Woodhall in Sandringham. Whether this was a wooden hall or the hall of the Wodes, or both at the same time, the transaction affords the first clue to a house on the site. Next, in 1327, Roger de Sandringham is found in possession. Men come and go but the land remains, and perhaps Roger is Sir Richard's son under another name.

The early records are broken and confused. We can suppose that the wooden hall was no doubt burned to the ground and rebuilt more than once. Possibly the lands were divided by inheritance into the two parcels of Woodhall and Westhall, farther west. For in his will dated August 16th 1447, Sir John Clifton directs that Westhall Manor, forming part of the three villages of Babingley, Wolferton and Sandringham, shall be sold and it appears that the purchaser was Thomas, Lord Scales.

This was the period of the Paston letters and, sure enough, Thomas Scales is found contributing several letters in the series, praying the "good judge, John Paston", that he "wyll fynde a waye accordyng to right" in disputes between tenants and neighbours.

Scales wrote from his family seat, Middleton Tower, to the south of Lynn, an imposing edifice he had built with materials salvaged from the demolition of a mansion at Castle Rising, owned by our acquaintances the Wodehouses. He was involved, however, on the losing side in the Wars of the Roses and in 1460, after striving to defend the Tower of London he was found murdered outside its walls. His estate passed to his daughter Elizabeth, the wife of Anthony Woodville, the second Earl Rivers, whose sister was Queen Elizabeth, consort of King Edward IV.

For the first time, Sandringham land is curiously close to the Royal Family. It is tempting to think that this first Elizabeth Regina, the first queen consort of the house of York, may have walked or at least visited the lands of Sandringham precisely five hundred years ago. The link with the Crown became still firmer when, in 1474, Elizabeth Scales died childless, leaving her husband in possession of her estates.

There was also another early link with the throne. Elizabeth Scales' father had woven the rich English traditions of the Pastons into the warp and woof of the Sandringham tapestry, and indeed the Pastons themselves owned land at Appleton. Now her sorrowing widower went on a pilgrimage to the shrine of St. James at Compostela and while on the voyage the idea occurred to him of translating a selection of various Greek authors from the existing French into English. So was produced "The Dictes or Sayengis of the Philosophers, a Translation out of Frenshe into Englyssh by the noble and puissant Lord Antone, Erl of Ryvers, Lord of Scales" which was printed in London by the newly-arrived William Caxton. Though not the first book printed by Caxton in England, it is the first dated book from his Westminster press.

We have progressed from the indecipherable parchments of Sandringham's lost past to the first printed records. In the British Museum is an illuminated painting on vellum of Earl Rivers presenting his printed book to Edward IV. He kneels at the King's feet, in a coat emblazoned with his heraldic quarterings, in blue stockings, his dark hair cut in a straight and modern fringe across his forehead.

This was his greatest hour of glory. Within six years, while conducting his nephew, the boy King Edward V, from Ludlow, Earl Rivers was arrested by order of Richard of Gloucester and soon afterwards executed. (He was uncle of both the young princes so mysteriously murdered in the Tower.) But some will think his greatest destiny after all was that he entered the imagination of Shakespeare as a ghost on Bosworth Field in Act V of *King Richard III*, rising in vengeance over his old enemy, "Let me sit heavy on thy soul tomorrow, Rivers, that died at Pomfret!"

His will bequeathing his Norfolk estates to his brother was never effected and the lands reverted to two of Elizabeth Scales' relatives, Lady Oxford and Sir William Tyndal.

By marriage the Cobbes had also risen as one of the leading Norfolk families, holding lands in Sandringham, Babingley, Wolferton, West Newton, Appleton and Anmer, and in 1517 the manor of Sandringham itself passed into their possession. And now the tide of change was stemmed within its boundaries, for the Catholic Cobbes contrived to survive the vicissitudes of both the Reformation and the Civil War and were to endure at Sandringham for 150 years.

II

There is a certain charm in discovering that in 1520, when King Henry VIII had still only one wife and had not met Anne Boleyn, "Mr. Cobbys and his wyff" set out from Sandringham to visit their neighbours, the L'Estranges at Hunstanton Hall, and there had for dinner a crane, six plover and a brace of rabbits. The Cobbe family had been locally known for two or three generations but they suddenly come to life, thanks to the remarkable preservation of the Tudor account books of Hunstanton Hall. The guests also included young Robert Brampton who married William Cobbe's sister. They crossed the moat and passed beside the noble entrance gatehouse that still stands to this day; they may have carried a gift of a piece of porpoise as the Cobbes were known to do on other occasions.

The accounts tell us that the Cobbes supplied wethers from their Dersingham sheep farm to the hospitable Hunstanton table: the gifts of pheasant and woodcock, the purchases of "candells, beffe, heryng and buttr" must have similarly figured in the accounts of Sandringham. We find that one young Cobbe meets and marries a Hunstanton guest who was a granddaughter of Sir John Spelman. A Cobbe girl similarly marries via Hunstanton into the Bedingfeld family and in the fulness of time her granddaughter marries back into the Cobbe family again.

It would be an unrewarding task to disentangle all these relationships but the skein becomes simpler when Sir William Cobbe, Knight — grandson, perhaps, of our earlier William — dies in 1581 and specially bequeaths to his sister Alice "one cup of silver-gilt, with a cover, which I bought at Lynn Mart, weighing between fifteen and sixteen ounces". Little did he dream how inundated with silver cups and other trophies Sandringham was one day to be!

The manor devolved upon his son, yet another William Cobbe, and it was he who married the cousin who had been a Bedingfeld as well as a Cobbe by descent. Her sister, Nazareth, married to a Yelverton, also lived near at hand in a "small house" at Wolferton. Once again there was a strong family group, knit all the closer by the secrecy and even terror of their staunch yet illegal Catholic faith.

In 1595 and thereabouts the name of Mary Cobbe and her sister both appear on the lists of Popish recusants who refused to attend the established Protestant worship at their parish church and were therefore liable to heavy fines and worse.

At Anmer old Christopher Walpole died of a heart attack after hearing that his Jesuit son had suffered torture and execution as a practising and unlicensed priest. The family at Sandringham lived in the shadow of this event and only William Cobbe's shrewd discretion in not avowing his conscience saved the estate from sequestration.

Though liable to search day and night, possibly the house was too small and the comings-and-goings of its residents too quiet and simple to attract suspicion. Local notoriety was more concerned with the new house which Sir Edward Paston was building not two miles away at Appleton, at the very gate of the Cobbes, "a very agreeable handsome pile", and "a very fair mansion", according to Norfolk topographers.

An avowed Protestant, Paston improved his fortune by methodically building on consecrated Popish ground which the Reformation had desecularised, but his conscience was less tough and more vulnerable than Cobbe's. A piece of half-demolished wall fell unexpectedly and killed a workman, and the accident so shocked Paston that he retired into Appleton and never built again.

Sir William Cobbe died in 1607, having presided over Sandringham for twenty-six years, and on to the scene comes his grandson, still another William Cobbe, the fourth or fifth, who flaunted both faith and loyalty with none of his grandsire's caution. Says Blomefield, the eighteenth-century Norfolk historian, "This William was a great royalist and a colonel in the army or militia, and suffered greatly on that account."

In 1643 Lynn declared itself royalist and was besieged by the Earl of Manchester with four thousand horse and foot. To the defence of the town rode the L'Estranges and Bedingfelds of Hunstanton and no doubt Cobbe and many others "on horseback, they and their men armed with swords and pistols". Royalist aid richly promised by the Earl of Newcastle turned out, however, to be merely one shipload of men and meagre provisions and, under threat of bombardment, the city fathers capitulated. Colonel Cobbe was not among the twenty-five signatories who impudently conjured Lord Manchester "that he should not forget to plunder them when he had taken the town". He was nevertheless reported "a Recusant and in arms against Parliament", and his Sandringham estates were totally sequestrated and the revenues appropriated for the use of the Commonwealth.

Seven years passed before Cobbe deemed it prudent to appeal. This was an expediency precipitated by two ruined tenants who had named him as "Papist and Delinquent", whereupon Cobbe promptly petitioned, "The petitioner's estate is sequestered, albeit no proof is or can be made against him for delinquency, neither is he convicted of Recusancy, however he humbly confesseth his Recusancy, and humbly praieth the allowance of a third of his estate with the mansion house. November 11, 1650."

The ways of the law were no faster then than now. A year later petitions were still being entered for his case to be examined. Among others, Colonel Cobbe persuaded the ambassador to the King of Spain to lodge an appeal on his behalf. This had some effect and in November 1652, the sequestration was discharged and his estate rights supposedly restored, yet, in 1653, an annuitant on the estate, Mary Cobbe, "being very aged and infirm" was praying that the Commissioners would be pleased to grant her an allowance.

The impoverishment of a decade of lost revenues was, however, to impress its dire effects even farther into the future. During the Cobbes' tenure, Sandringham had been "peopled and enlivened over and over again by an enormous family of children", becoming in due course an enormous army of relatives and dependents, steadily diminishing the family nest-egg without replenishment. Of Colonel Cobbe's five daughters, four took the veil in foreign convents, where they died. Two of his sons became priests, a fourth son left no children and the third son, Geoffrey, inherited Sandringham in 1665.

Of his tenure, we know only that the land was let "quit and free of passage, tallage, payage, lastage, stalage, portage, pesage and terrage" — free, that is, of road tolls, certain taxes to the Crown, shipping freight tax, market rent for stalls and other dues. The estate also provided fuel for an Admiralty beacon that flamed on the Sandringham heights to guide shipping to Lynn. As if alarmed by the troubled events that marked the short reign of James II, Geoffrey Cobbe sold Sandringham in 1686 but he had an only child, Elizabeth, who was alive in 1727 to help confide to the printed page some of the memories of her home.

III

Sandringham is widely regarded today as characteristically English, its way of life the quintessence of the English tradition yet, curiously, its owners in the last three centuries have twice stemmed from foreign refugee stock.

James Hoste, English-born son of a London merchant, purchased Sandringham in 1686, having settled in the neighbourhood some eight years earlier. His grandfather, Jacques Hoost, was a Dutchman who fled from Middleburg in the Netherlands at the height of the Protestant persecutions. It is an apposite turning of the tables that the Cobbes, having held Sandringham for 150 years and endured the oppression of the Protestants, should be fated to be succeeded for the next 150 years by the sturdy Hostes who had suffered far more from the hideous cruelty of the Catholic Duke of Alva.

The blood of the Hostes was no less ancient. When Sir Richard de la Rokele built perhaps the first wooden manorhouse of Sandringham, the Hoosts were already respectably inscribed in the municipal records of Bruges, and when Roger de Sandringham held possession a Hoost was a sheriff of that city.

Jacques Hoost arrived in London in 1569 to receive, on naturalisation, the addition of wings to his coat of arms in allusion to his flight and a pair of wings for his family crest. But this was not his only memento, for he also brought or subsequently retrieved a double-clasped Bible and a painted portrait of a young Flemish kinswoman who had been burned at the stake. Alva poured upon the Protestants of the Netherlands the terror which Hitler reserved for the Jews. We are told that tens of thousands went "to the stake, the sword, the gallows, the living grave" and among his victims was this girl, with her bovine eyes and pouting lips, her portrait enshrining the story of "the Flemish Martyr" that vividly persisted at Sandringham for 250 years and more after her death.

The Bible depicted beneath her placid hand was the same heavy twin-buckled volume which Jacques Hoost carried into exile, a book regarded with veneration and passed down as a sacred relic from one generation to the next. Like leaves in their seasons, the English-born James Hoste was succeeded by his son and then his grandson of the same name.

Primed with his merchant fortune, the first James not only acquired Sandringham but also rose in the year 1704 to be Sheriff of Norfolk, an official role in which he was shocked to receive a writ for royal dues which the town had neglected to pay.

Three years later the moated grandeur of Appleton Hall came to an end when the house was burned to the ground one night and "the family had all like to have burnt in their beds if a shepherd had not waked them". The fugitives were no doubt brought shivering to Sandringham in the early hours and that night Sandringham became, as it has since remained, the prime house of the immediate neighbourhood. The Pastons moved away and James Hoste II subsequently added the lands of Appleton to his own.

We have a precise tradition, too, of the Sandringham manorhouse of those days. An enthusiastic Norfolk notetaker, Peter le Neve, probably had it from the lips of Elizabeth Cobbe and it was later embalmed in the Victorian prose of the conscientious (if occasionally inaccurate) local historian, Mrs. Herbert Jones. Sandringham was then "a long low house, with wings and rather small windows" and it was perhaps the second James who enlarged it for his growing family, only to forget the staircase in the alterations "so that it had to be awkwardly inserted in the roof of the hall".

The oversight no doubt provided a rich anecdote for his son, the third James, who became a Member of Parliament and was devoted to good talk and gossip. Indeed, almost the only knowledge we have of James Hoste, M.P., of Sandringham Hall, is a brief neighbourly glimpse in 1743 when he scribbled a letter to the Dersingham parson, enclosing a copy of the *Extraordinary Gazette*, almost audibly smacking his lips over some local news item.

James Hoste the second had married first Elizabeth Walpole, who died childless, and then an Ann Burleigh, and from their second son, Theodore, there descended the Sir William Hoste who served under Nelson and commanded a brig at the Battle of the Nile. His career was furthered, needless to say, by Nelson's own Norfolk background, and when William Hoste was only seventeen Nelson forecast in a letter that he would be an honour to Norfolk and to England and so it proved.

It became a sore point with Captain Hoste that he missed Trafalgar. "Not to have been in it is enough to make one mad," he wrote. "I am low indeed, and nothing but a good action with a French or Spanish frigate will set me up again". Such a letter may well have found its way to his Sandringham cousins although the adventurous seafarer had to wait six years for the action that glowed in his imagination. When it came, in 1811, in the Gulf of Venice, his four ships were pitted against eight vessels of the French and Venetian squadron crewed with thrice the number of men. The redoubtable Hoste commenced the action with a signal, "Remember Nelson". The English sailors rose to the slogan and in six hours the action was won.

But by then a new family unit occupied Sandringham, more remote in kinship and headed by Henry Hoste Henley. The old folk were gone. Many more changes had passed under the wheel of eighty years. The third James Hoste was survived by an only daughter, Susan, and like Elizabeth Scales three centuries earlier, Susan was the sole heiress of Sandringham when — in August 1752 — she married Cornish Henley of Leigh House, Somerset. They were both twenty-two years of age and must have made an attractive couple.

IV

With a bride of his own age, her untrammelled fortune and the vast estate, Cornish Henley was, of course, in clover. He elected to live exclusively at Sandringham. Indeed, he viewed the property with a new and lively eye. The Great Bustard still frequented the neighbourhood, the rivers teemed with trout, the woods abounded in game, and Henley appears to have been the first to develop his lands with a watchful regard to the promising sport.

He had not been married three years when he entered into an agreement with William Mason of Necton for keeping up a joint pack of hounds, the pack being a month at Necton and a month at Sandringham alternately throughout the season. This saw the establishment of fox hunting in Norfolk as a regular institution, and also assuredly saw the entertainment at Sandringham of the eccentric third Earl of Orton, whose whole pleasure was "outrageous exercise", and who appeared at every meet in a fierce cocked hat, facing every wind that blew "mounted on a stump of a piebald pony (as broad as he was long) in a full suit of black, without either great-coat or gloves; his hands and face crimsoned with cold".

Spending thousands a year in falconry, Orton's hawks must have been a great nuisance to his country neighbours, not least the Henleys. For social gatherings he was apt to arrive at

Cornish Henley's hospitable door with the four red-dear stags he had trained to run in a phaeton, though Sandringham happily did not see the memorable incident when his peculiar team was chased by a pack of hounds and the "mad Earl", his stags and equipage, managed to take refuge in a barn only just ahead of the hounds.

But these were the days of the innovator. Touring Norfolk in 1770, Arthur Young, the agriculturist, found Cornish engrossed in lively experiment. "About Sandringham, the seat of Henry Cornish Henley, Esq. are very considerable tracts of sandy land, which are applied at present only to the feeding of rabbits. It is a very barren soil but not, I apprehend, incapable of cultivation: it lets from 1s. 6d. to 2s. 6d. an acre in warrens. Mr. Henley has tried some experiments on it lately, with a view to discover how far it will answer cultivating. The value of it is prodigiously advanced by planting. That gentleman has formed several plantations, which thrive extremely; all the firs do well, and will pay a better rent for the land than any husbandry."

Cornish Henley was, in fact, as representative as he could be of the hard-riding, hard-drinking and enterprising Georgian squirearchy, those robust, often eccentric apostles of individualism who brought such colour and vigour to the rural core of the eighteenth century. He bent his mind to agriculture as he bent his mind to the arts. He rode well and read well. He was the all-round man, and if he still found much beyond his reach there was little at least beyond attempting.

This was the age when the Leicesters were still completing the Palladian glories of Holkham Hall and Capability Brown was landscaping the grounds of Holkham at fifty guineas a visit. William Windham II had scarcely emerged from the pangs of rebuilding at Felbrigg with all the delay of tardy stonemasons and the goading absurdity of the architect "sending a plasterer who could not do Ornaments".

Although Horace Walpole, "the most fastidious of men" did not often visit his embellished family home at Houghton, he represented first Castle Rising and then Lynn as a Member of Parliament, and Cornish Henley was sufficiently within his social orbit in Norfolk to be inspired by his sparkling architectural enthusiasm. "On Friday we went to see — oh, the palace of palaces! ... such expense! such taste! such profusion!... The old house ... so improved and enriched that all the Percies and Seymours of Sion must die of envy... There is a hall, library, breakfast-room, eating-room, all chefs-d'oeuvre of Adam, a gallery one hundred and thirty feet long, and a drawing-room worthy of Eve before the Fall."

So wrote Horace Walpole after visiting Osterley some years after the events we chronicle. It was an era when gentlemen went sightseeing to the great houses, Wilton, Longleat, Knole. In any case, England was swept with an explosive passion for building in the new styles — first admiration and then emulation — and Cornish Henley impetuously adopted this fervour for improvement.

He was sufficiently up-to-date to dream of a house clothed completely in stucco. The carefree family finances imposed no limit of size. A single range of reception rooms was not enough and he placed a second range beside them. Two storeys did not suffice for nursery and service needs and so Henley cheerfully allowed himself a third floor of ample attics. His wife, too, was certainly his happy accomplice in every extravagance.

Although her money pleasantly helped to build the larger, grander Sandringham — the self-same house bought many decades later by the Prince of Wales — Susan Hoste Henley could ardently follow fashion. This was at about the time when Horace Walpole discovered that at Battle Abbey "a miss of the family" had "clothed a fragment of the portico with cockle-shells" and Susan Henley also followed the craze of collecting seashells for decor, the souvenirs of many a happy summer afternoon.

It might be said that the second Duchess of Richmond and her daughters took seven years to complete their Shell House at Goodwood in the 1740's, in spite of the assistance of the Royal Navy in collecting shells in the West Indies. The Countess of Tyrone also triumphantly completed a grotto complete with her own statue and the inscription "In two hundred and sixty one days these shells were put up by the proper hands of the Rt. Honourable Catherine Countess of Tyrone, 1754". Susan Henley, in her rustic seclusion, trailed a little behind these aristocratic exemplars, although with her young son, Henry, to assist in the pastime she went one better than Lady Tyrone by lining an entire room at Sandringham with seashells.

Though neither Cornish nor his architect could hope to equal the Earl of Leicester's great house, the exterior style of the new Henley house bore a vague resemblance to Holkham. Was Henley perhaps envious of the Holkham library? He soon had a library of his own, filled, we are told, with "curious volumes, among them French illuminated books". The vogue for plaster work had begun and the ceilings were not without delicate rococo fancies. There were rooms "hung with genre pictures". The shell room, too, was occupied by a company of stuffed bears, lions and tigers, as if in rivalry to the Duke of Richmond's menagerie and the aviary "full of birds from a thousand islands" that Walpole noted at Osterley. This short-lived "middle Sandringham", the eighteenth-century mansion linking the old manorhouse with the royal home of today, was doomed to last less than a century and is not well documented.

The sole surviving estate map of Henley days in the Sandringham estate office sheds no light on the order of building.

When Cornish Henley first came to Sandringham local legend suggests that he found a rambling house built to an Elizabethan plan around three sides of a square. The repeated pattern of stucco gables in his new home indicate that, when he demolished the old house, he forthwith built two ranges side by side. But one certainty is that Henley indulged himself with a long gallery, running the whole length of the house between the two sets of reception rooms, a feature that also appealed to later taste and still influences the ground plan of royal Sandringham.

Cornish Henley, however, probably did not live to see the full completion of his plans. He died in 1773, when he was forty-one years old, leaving his widow to finish the reconstruction. His only son, Henry Hoste Henley, was then a boy of eight. As a young man he may have been responsible for the additions that altered and irretrievably ruined the architect's original ideal. Otherwise our only evidence of his romantic caprice is that he refronted Babingley manorhouse with "gingerbread" carstone and thus erased the testimony of three hundred years.

No doubt he acted on high motives and was attempting to bring the place into line with the architectural patternbooks of 1820. Henry and his wife had two grown sons, Francis and George, and two daughters, Lucy and Sarah, any one of whom may have qualified for a house at about this time. But Lucy and Sarah both died in 1826 and none of the children survived their twenties. The flat tombstones of the Henleys half pave the northern side of the Sandringham churchyard.

Writing sixty years later, Mrs. Herbert Jones drew on fading remembrances handed down from 1820 to tell us of a room called the kitchen chamber, a bedroom over the kitchen, where Henry Hoste Henley had stored his unwanted family pictures, including "a number of old Dutch portraits, apparently put there to be out of the way, piled against the wall in the unused room". Among them was the old painting of the Flemish Martyr in her plain black gown of thick texture, her lace cap and cuffs and great white ruff, gazing implacably at her neglected world.

The servants of the house used to steal up to the chamber to gaze at her in awe and they shunned her superstitiously when twilight descended. And now she vanishes, her Bible lost with her despite all the unremitting years of care, though the portrait was at one time reported to be in the possession of a Colonel Henley at Leigh in Somerset.

Henry Hoste Henley died on St. George's Day in his sixty-eighth year in 1833. His nearest kinsfolk were his Somerset cousins. They removed the pictures and, after some delay, an auction sale took place which dispersed the "miscellaneous collections and the rest of the household furniture among the neighbouring halls and rectories".

Sallies and laughter no doubt greeted the stuffed animals, though they may have proved a bargain to some travelling showman. The house is emptied, the servants bid one another farewell, "the last wagon-wheels, low on the sand and loud on the stone, finally echo away". It is difficult to refrain from sentiment as the silence falls and the deserted house gapes at another night.

3: MR. MOTTEUX'S PURCHASE

I

The departure of Henry Hoste Henley from the scene brought a pause in the chain of domestic consequence that had throbbed through Sandringham for 150 years. The tumbling waters of consecutive event were held for three years at the placid weir of the auction room. Yet in the year 1686, when the Cobbes relinquished their hold and the manorhouse was acquired by the Hostes, another immigrant tributary had also begun its flow towards the mainstream of Sandringham history.

The Hostes had fled from Flanders moving irresistibly towards Sandringham in the tidal force of religious persecution, and in this other tributary the current of events was precisely repeated. The revocation of the edict of Nantes saw civil rights withdrawn from French Protestants and in the stampede of Huguenot refugees across the Channel there came one, Pierre Anthony Motteux, the son of a Rouen merchant. A vigorous, heartwhole young man of twenty-five, he found the risks of the sea-passage and of being smuggled ashore no more than a lively day's adventure, and he quickly established himself in the silk trade.

Four years later, William and Mary signed their declaration of protection, "We do hereby declare that all French Protestants that shall seek their refuge in this our kingdom shall not only have our royal protection for themselves, families and estates, within this our realm, but we will also do our endeavour in all reasonable ways and means so to support, aid and assist them…"

Under this warrant Pierre's nephew, John Motteux, stepped in safety onto an English quay, claiming a new land as his own and never dreaming that his name would one day come to be engrossed on its royal title-deeds.

We can watch this youngster making his way to his uncle's new warehouse in Leadenhall Street where "the family lived over the shop". We can watch him rubbing his eyes at the wares from China and Japan there displayed, the "pictures, tea, fans, muslins, gold and silver brocades and foreign silks…"

Only his name, indeed, immediately concerns us, borne by his father before him and destined to be the name of his grandson the purchaser of Sandringham from Hoste Henley's executors. Uncle Pierre had Anglicised his name to "Peter" and hung the elegant sign of "The Two Fans" over the door of his establishment. Thereupon a whole brood of Motteux youngsters proceeded to make it the rendezvous of wealth and fashion, chiefly by the method, not unknown to publicists, of telling all and sundry that it was so.

Young John Motteux became naturalised by royal letters patent in 1693 and went into the business, together with brothers and cousins who no doubt staggered into the store with many a load from the nearby India Company and unpacked fabrics for enticing display. Having thus put some of his mercantile tasks on to younger shoulders, Peter Motteux branched out into pursuits he found more personally congenial, such as devising advertisements, editing *The Gentleman's Journal* and translating the complete works of Rabelais in six volumes.

This was an astute and characteristic move, for a translation already existed by another hand. Motteux had but to revise part to make three books and directly translate only three volumes from the French. Moreover, the reading public for rumoured pornography was as avid then as now. His name thus steadily before the public as the volumes appeared, Peter next turned to play-writing. In the modern view of Professor Sampson, they were "plays without the smallest distinction", but the pieces were produced at a theatre in Lincoln's Inn Fields with such a level of approval that Dryden readily composed a poetic prelude to perhaps the best of them, *Beauty in Distress*. In this Motteux had the benefit of Mrs. Bracegirdle playing the sorrows and triumphs of the heroine.

"She was of a lovely height," wrote a devotee, "and whenever she exerted herself had an involuntary flushing in her breast, neck and face." Scarce an audience saw her, we are told further, that were not half of them her lovers.

The versatile Motteux then composed musical interludes and masques, among them an *Acis and Galatea* some years ahead of the celebrated version by Gay and Handel. In 1700 he made a translation of *Don Quixote* direct from the Spanish and it is on record that Carey Coke added a copy to the library at Holkham. Is it too wishful to suppose that it may have been lent to James Hoste at Sandringham? Mrs. Coke at all events made so much of her first volume that Motteux dedicated a second volume to her husband.

The Huguenot knew how to make the most of his friends: the trait was in his blood. Addison and Steele's *Spectator* no sooner grew into the life of London than Motteux became a minor contributor. Meanwhile he was still sending out catalogues of the pictures and other new goods of his Leadenhall Street warehouse and his City reputation as "the Chinaman" remained undimmed. It was rather as if Noël Coward were running Harrods. When the theatrical world was quiet, he wrote verse as advertising copy in praise of his commodities:

The panacea you should boast is Tea…
Chaste, yet not cold; and sprightly, yet not wild,
Tho' gentle, strong, and tho' compulsive, mild…

Unfortunately, his own preference was a stronger brew. Leaving his wife at home with the teapot, we catch a last glimpse of him setting out in a hackney coach, dressed in long scarlet cloak with hat and sword, to celebrate his fifty-eighth birthday with boon companions elsewhere. The party was a wild one, the roisterers staged a mock hanging and just as Peter Motteux was "hanged up in sport" a noisy procession chanced to pass the windows. Rushing to look at it, they momentarily forgot the dangling birthday boy and when they returned the playwright was dead.

He left seven children, the eldest only in her teens, but the warehouse continued to thrive under his nephew, John Motteux, and others of the family. Of an equable yet no less enterprising temperament, John helped to erect the Huguenot hospital for the aged and poor and when he died, apparently as a result of indiscreet Christmas feasting, in 1741, the prosperous family East India business was still thriving in Walbrook.

His successor, his son, John, was, however, only four years old. And so once again the players wait in the Sandringham wings until, in early middle age, mistakenly scenting business perils in the difficulties of Warren Hastings in the Indian wars, this further John shrewdly bought himself land at Beachamwell to the south-east of King's Lynn.

Here he found himself the father of a desolate Norfolk hamlet which was little better than a collection of hovels mustered around a thatch-roofed Norman church and a forge; he left it a model village of twenty-two cottages built of local brick, with a stately hall, fertile acres and a well-ordered church

54

on a two-acre green, a precept of the most civilised eighteenth-century ideal.

Urbane architecture was also only one of his interests. In the church is a finely wrought-iron chest which John Motteux designed, it is said to provide work at his forge in a slack period. When he died in 1793, his villagers and friends with loving regard accorded him the finest funeral the county had ever witnessed, a funeral still remembered as "gorgeous" by the old men sixty years afterwards.

John Motteux had also first rented and then purchased the estate of Banstead Place in Surrey, which he bequeathed to his second son, Robert, while the eldest — inevitably named John — was left Beachamwell. Both sons were to share his London house in Walbrook and both were prudently left instructions for carrying on the firm. Robert also received the specific sum of £30,000, while his two sisters were each left £15,000.

These later Motteuxs were the last withered apples on the tree, for they never married. Robert built himself a new red-brick house, "a model erection", at Banstead Place and settled down with his two sisters to enjoy the fruit of its 360 acres, the "good gardens and hothouse and greenhouse, the paddocks and prospects and coppice". It was John, probably Norfolk born and bred, who carried affairs the final step towards Sandringham.

II

John Motteux — brother of Robert — greatly increased his fortune by army contracts during the Napoleonic wars, a secret he was afterwards conveniently inclined to keep to himself. The high price of wheat in those years handsomely recouped Beachamwell expenditure. He planted trees to improve the estate, including the great sycamore on the village green, and he established the village school, an institution that itself proved most serviceable when he entertained large shooting parties, filling his house with guests, and could order the schoolchildren "to be distributed about, to brush the coverts, like so many spaniels".

An undersized man in a company of stalwart Englishmen, John Motteux in fact missed few moves in the strategy of improving his social position. He was a frequent guest at Woburn and Holkham and through Coke of Holkham, whom he had known since boyhood, he had been appointed Sheriff of Norfolk. Staying with his own relatives at Banstead Place, moreover, he made the acquaintance of their neighbour, a Mrs. Spencer who resided in the old manorhouse that had been lushly renamed Banstead Park.

As an astute widow, Mrs. Spencer may have failed with the younger brother and hopefully ogled the older John, "a short man, rather stout, with large whiskers, a commonplace manner and most unideal aspect", but her plans were not destined to blossom in romance. And yet the effect was romantic, firing as it did another spark in the train of circumstance that directly led to the royal ownership of Sandringham House.

Through Mrs. Spencer at Banstead, John Motteux met her kinsman, the fifth Earl Cowper, a wealthy and influential Whig, close to the government, and thus a contact to be sedulously cultivated. In social life, Earl Cowper was nevertheless a stodge, put in the shade by his wilful, witty, vivacious and extremely pretty young wife. He was relieved to sit back while Motteux kept the ball-game of conversation going, perhaps wistful with admiration when "the little Huguenot" met Emmy Cowper's sallies with his own "dry remarks and good humour".

We are told that Motteux was soon the Cowpers "constant guest". Though Emmy led an absorbing social life, she bore her husband five children — although it was whispered that some were Palmerston's — and Motteux entered this warm if irregular family circle in time — at fifty — to dandle the youngest boy, George Spencer, on his knee.

Lady Cowper in turn opened the doors of exclusive Almack's and introduced the Huguenot to the brilliant literary circle of Holland House, where Motteux still had wit and facility enough to hold his own. When George IV came to the throne, it was perhaps Motteux who gossiped to Lady Holland that the Cowpers had "dined twice with the King and he has persuaded them to stay another week". At all events, the news of this royal hospitality delighted them both.

Another story has come down of a warm discussion between the redoubtable Lady Holland and Mr. Motteux on whether prunes should form an ingredient in cock-a-leekie soup. Motteux kept a French cook at his own mansion and rightly maintained that French plums or prunes should be used to flavour veal soup or cock-a-leekie, both one and the same. Motteux relished his food and was reported by Harriet, Countess Granville, when in Paris "to eat of sixteen entrees every day".

He was, however, unfortunate, in his chefs. His French cook gambled away the money entrusted him for discharging the tradesmen's accounts and then messily committed suicide. Another cook at Beachamwell was suddenly taken seriously ill on the morning of a large shooting party. Motteux sent post-haste for the doctor and was overheard to instruct him, "Bolster him up for a few hours *till the dinner is served* and then let him die as soon as he likes!"

The story was soon all over town. Though amusing, it gives a false picture of Motteux, who later left each of his servants a handsome legacy and annuity, and the laughter rolled off his back. He was as immune to ridicule as to snubs. He did not in the least mind being misrepresented, whether as "a retired silk merchant" or, worse, "an Italian mountebank".

To encourage talk, indeed, he was capable of large extravagant gestures, greeting an approaching marriage on one occasion by producing a twist of silver paper from his pocket and flinging it down on the table, full of unset diamonds of great value, as a gift to the bride. He enjoyed the aura of mystification, as he enjoyed life.

We see him for a moment in a letter from Countess Granville to Lady Carlisle when France was welcoming the return of Louis Philippe, "Paris, July 29, 1831. Friday morning, balcon of the Hotel Bristol, chez Monsieur Motteux. A beautiful sight, day blue and gold, the Place cleared of the populace, but every window and balcon full. The King on a white horse with his sons. Pedro with all his green feathers rode up to the Queen's balcon, like a tourney, Lady Carlisle…" We see him at a dinner party with the Cowpers and Talleyrand, discoursing so vigorously on one of his pet enthusiasms that the French ambassador turns with curiosity to his hostess, "And who is this little gentleman *with his mania for pears*?"

In private, indeed, Mr. Motteux cultivated his garden. In 1826 he won the Large Silver Medal of the Horticultural Society, of which he was an early member, "for the Cultivation of Fruits in his garden at Beachamwell, as proved by his frequent exhibition of its produce to the Society".

Mr. Motteux's cultivated Marie Louise pears were so luscious, so superb to look at as well as eat, that the Society engaged an artist to depict a sample for their annual volume. A fig, which he covered in with glass, was no less celebrated for its luxuriance and fertility. Unhappily, the death of his two sisters deprived him of the pleasure of reporting his triumphs in the family circle where no doubt he enjoyed telling them best.

The Cowper children, however, were growing up to munch his pears under his eyes, and Motteux was a droll and sympathetic spectator watching all the signs of the secret love affair deepening between Emmy and Lord Palmerston. In 1834 the latter was instrumental in procuring a clerkship in the Foreign Office as an opening to George Spencer Cowper, Mr. Motteux's own favourite protégé.

It was two years after this, on an early summer day at Beachamwell, that Motteux opened his newspaper and discovered with intense interest that the Sandringham Hall estate was announced for sale at long last. "...an estate of magnitude and proportion, equally desirable for residence or investment, situated in one of the finest sporting districts, regularly hunted by the Norfolk foxhounds and harriers, with a mansion placed in a deer-park of considerable extent, altogether constituting with Manors and Advowsons 5,450 acres of land, lying within a ring fence."

We can be sure that Mr. Motteux read on, thoughtfully digesting the details, "...a Mansion and domestic offices, placed on a lawn and surrounded by a deer park and pleasure grounds 340 acres in extent, varied with ornamental oak and other thriving timber and plantations, approached by a carriage drive through a beautiful plantation and avenue of lime, firs and other forest trees. The park commanding pleasing and interesting views of the surrounding country, enclosed by a stone wall and park palings.

"The above domain", the notice continued, "is situated in a perfectly dry and salubrious district and is unrivalled in proportion to its extent for the rearing and preservation of game which abound in all their varieties.

"There is also a heronry on the estate, fish ponds and sheets of water, well stocked with fresh water fish, and the Castle Rising river forms the southern boundary of the property, excepting one mile" — here the author had clearly pulled himself together — "excepting one mile which runs through the estate, thereby securing the exclusive rights of fishing in one of the finest trout streams in the kingdom.

"The southern boundary of the estate is only 5 miles from King's Lynn, 14 from Swaffham and adjoins the estate of the Hon. Colin Howard. The woods and plantations which contain 310 acres in addition to park and plantations of 340 acres, bring the total to 650 acres. The remainder of the estate, farms and cottages, being let to respectable tenants at extremely low rents. The parochial rates do not amount to more than 9d. per acre. The Turnpike road for London runs through the estate. Cards to view from Mr. Jarvis, solicitor, Lynn; T. E. Clarke, solicitor, Chard; Clovery and Woodlake, solicitors in King's Bench Walk."

Mr. Motteux was, of course, as well acquainted with Sandringham as with his own London mansion in Stratford Place or with the closer neighbouring estates around Swaffham. In that tight-knit remote countryside he would frequently have enjoyed Henry Hoste Henley's hospitality, with other local gentry. He had often shot over the estate if not enjoyed its trout-fishing. There was no need for Mr. Motteux to seek cards to view when a coin would open doors far wider and faster.

In all probability, he had awaited the date of the auction with some impatience and may have already made an offer through a discreet nominee or tested the anticipated value by some other means. Through his own quiet and devious inquiries, he would have assessed precisely the strength of competition that the auction was likely to sustain.

The Notice of Sale contained nothing new except the date and place: on July 19th 1836, at the Auction Mart in London. And there, in the crowded and airless rooms, with the familiar figure of Mr. W. W. Simpson on the rostrum, the Sandringham Hall Estate was sold "after spirited competition" to Mr John Motteux for £76,000.

Mr. Motteux's motive in the purchase can be only conjectured. In his lifetime he had seen the wastes around Beachamwell profitably sown with wheat until the lands were yielding £20,000 a year. In his seventieth year Mr. Motteux may have been moved to repeat his father's example of fuller investment in property. Perhaps the approach of old age, too, drew the two brothers, John and Robert, closer together and they wished their rural interests to be less apart than Banstead and Beachamwell. Robert did not attend the auction, for he had been absent in Paris. Hurrying home to 7 Stratford Place, lively with victory, Mr. Motteux must have been drafting the very phrases of the letter he would promptly dispatch to Robert to convey the good news. But the letter was destined never to be sent and it was probably never written.

In the hour of John Motteux's triumph fate struck him its most desperate blow. He can scarcely have entered the house than news was brought to him that Robert had died in Paris five days earlier and was about to be interred in the cemetery of Père Lachaise. At a stroke John Motteux owned

Beachamwell and Sandringham and Banstead, all three, as the bitter and empty outcome of his plans.

III

John Motteux never lived at Sandringham, it is said that he never furnished it, though he planted pear trees and visited them attentively, awaiting the appetising harvest of their fruit.

He had owned the place barely a year when fate dealt him a fresh blow in the death of his old friend, Earl Cowper. Putting an end to lavish entertainment, Mr. Motteux sold his Stratford Place mansion and took a smaller house in Gloucester Place, although the move was premature: there was still Emmy, in genuine and self-reproachful mourning, to console and the affairs of her children, the eldest now themselves married with new bevies of cherubs to engage his affections.

The festivities of Queen Victoria's accession year coincided with George Spencer Cowper's coming-of-age. The old family friend clucked indulgently if he found a wayward and even spendthrift streak in the young man.

Spencer had advanced from his Foreign Office clerkship and was now private secretary to Lord Palmerston; he had taken to playing cards at Crockford's, a "bad thing" that even the Queen knew about, but he would settle down and, with proper endowment, he might one day rise to the highest political rank. There were a few delicious hours, indeed, when Spencer by proxy placed Motteux beside the throne. Sarah, Lady Lyttelton, herself related to the Cowpers, recorded in February 1839 a family occasion with the Queen at Buckingham Palace. "A great dinner yesterday (twenty-two). The Dowager Lady Cowper (Emmy), Lady Fanny Cowper, Mr. Spencer Cowper, Mr. William Cowper, Lady Ashley (née Cowper)… Coopers enough to mend all the butts and hogs-heads in the world!" It scarcely mattered that Palmerston, as Foreign Minister, so long in love with Emmy, had the best of personal reasons first for advancing her youngest son and then for placing him diplomatically out of the way.

Partly as a result of the Queen's observant eye at table and partly on Palmerston's recommendation, Spencer was appointed secretary of the legation in Florence but delayed his departure long enough to attend his mother's marriage to Palmerston at St. George's, Hanover Square.

The wedding of the fifty-year-old Emmy and the statesman five years her senior evidently provided Mr. Motteux with a new lease of life. He began ringing Sandringham with new boundary stones inscribed "I.M.1839" and lost no opportunity of improving the estate by fresh purchases. He could make guests smile again by vehemently maintaining that he had taken no medicine throughout all his lifetime and no corrective save lemon juice, and it seemed indeed that his energies might go on for ever. He added at least another thousand acres to Sandringham in the next four years.

Meanwhile, in 1841, he was similarly occupied in rounding off the Banstead property and early in 1843 he embarked on renovations at Beachamwell so extensive that, with three other houses to occupy, he was driven strangely to take lodgings in Lynn itself.

There occurred the notable occasion when he went to attend Divine Service one Sunday at St. Nicholas Church and thoughtlessly seated himself in an empty pew only to be politely asked to move. The family who paid the customary pew rents had arrived and he was obliged to seek another place. But here, too, he was no sooner seated than the customary occupants arrived and he was summarily ejected.

This led Mr. Motteux to make earnest inquiries into the church seating in Lynn from which he discovered that the existing three thousand seats allowed room for not one fifth of the population. Thereupon he gave £1,500 towards the erection of a new church with free sittings and Mr. Salvin was called in to design a church in Early English style. The Marquis of Cholmondeley, Lord George Bentinck, the Corporation of Lynn and others contributed to an additional £3,000.

The District Church of St. John, though unfurnished, was consecrated on June 14th 1843. And this lively show of enterprise was not a moment too soon for, six weeks later, on July 30th, John Motteux in turn was gathered to his fathers.

IV

"Poor Motteux!" said old Lady Holland. But when the will was read and she heard its astonishing terms from Lady Palmerston she immediately dashed off a letter to her son. "Mr. Motteux has left Spencer Cowper heir to all his immense fortune. I am not surprised. He was so like his father, Lord Cowper, who was Motteux's greatest friend, and the young man was also a great personal favourite. The wealth is very great. Spencer is charming. You must remember how much he was at Holland House, and how much we liked him. This gives me great pleasure."

This was not fully accurate, for the bequest was only of Mr. Motteux's landed property in Norfolk with the exception of £10,000 given in legacies and annuities, but the fortune was great enough.

Fashionable London buzzed with the news. But Spencer Cowper was then secretary of the Legation in Stockholm and the story goes that he could detect the invariably ominous content of a solicitor's letter by the handwriting and sealing-wax. The solicitor's letter intended to acquaint him with his good fortune reached him in mid-August. Unpleasantly aware of debts unpaid in London, Spencer looked at the envelope and laid it aside unopened, with a shudder.

Three weeks passed before the puzzling stream of congratulations from other correspondents impelled him to examine the letter closer. He resigned from the foreign service on the spot.

Back in England, the safe but dull farmlands of Beachamwell were of little appeal, the sporting prospects of Sandringham seemed far more alluring, but Spencer dutifully erected a tablet in the Beachamwell church to his benefactor, before he sold Beachamwell, donated £500 to the new church in King's Lynn, and then blithely rented a London town house from the Duke of Argyll.

Going to dinner there some six months later Lady Holland found him nobly ensconced "in his pretty house," as she confided to her son. "He lives very handsomely without profusion, not with vulgar profusion like a parvenu. All is in good taste, the plate beautiful; poor Motteux's crest, a bird, has a very pretty effect on the tops of the dishes. The cellars are abundantly stored with the best of wines, very choice and excellent. He now only wants a suitable wife to make him perfectly happy; for his eye I believe to be very safe."

But a safe eye, either for women or investments, was precisely what Spencer Cowper did not possess. He divided his time between London, Paris and his neglected country estate. Sandringham no doubt witnessed many uproarious bachelor parties during the forties and it was not until 1852, when he was thirty-six years old, that Spencer Cowper elected to marry a lady four years his senior, Lady Harriet d'Orsay, the widow of Count Alfred d'Orsay. And now we must retrace our steps to consider the strange story next destined to fall into place in the Sandringham frame.

In 1809, then — at the time when Lieutenant Henry Hoste Henley was training the militia in case Napoleon should land an army in Norfolk — the heir to the earldom of Blessington took a seaside villa as a cosy nest for himself and a certain Mrs. Brown in Worthing.

Three years later, when this lady learned of her husband's death, he married her in time to bestow legitimacy on their third child, Harriet, and the following year on a son. The advent of the little boy seems, however, to have caused the death of his mother, and the orphaned children were brought up by a Dublin aunt.

Harriet was seven years old before being presented to a new stepmama, a former Mrs. Farmer, who had been her father's solace for some time, and the child was too young to realise that the marriage was due to the alcoholism of Captain Farmer, who had considerately fallen out of a window and broken his neck.

Lord Blessington had now come into his title and his fortune and, travelling about Europe, alternately with and without Harriet and the other children, the prodigal Blessington caravan invariably caused a sensation This notoriety increased when the family settled in Naples in 1823 and the household was found to include the young and exquisite Count Alfred d'Orsay, "the model of all that could be conceived of noble demeanour and youthful candour, the beau ideal of manly dignity and grace with a gaiety of heart that spread happiness on all around".

With vivid memories of Sir William Hamilton and Lady Hamilton and Horatio Nelson, Neapolitan society regarded the piquant pattern as being repeated. Since no one knew that d'Orsay was the son of a hairdresser who had bought the small estate and titles of d'Orsay during the Revolution, the elegant Count was accepted at his own high face value as a sculptor, artist, dancer, fencer, swimmer, runner, horseman and beau ideal.

Lord Blessington seems not to have known of the rumours that surrounded his beautiful wife and her young friend or, if he did, he brushed them aside. His only son, a delicate boy of ten, died during that visit to Italy and, under this sorrow, Blessington devised a will which he imagined would protect his wife and daughter, and yet weave Alfred d'Orsay as an unassailable guardian figure to look after them both within the continued fabric of family life.

Lady Blessington was left an annuity of £3,000 a year. Harriet was to receive the estates in Dublin, with £10,000, provided she married Alfred d'Orsay. Within twelve months of the marriage, Alfred was to receive the annual interest on £20,000 and on his death Harriet would receive an annual interest on £40,000, while various clauses covered the other children and other contingencies.

The will might have become a paradise for lawyers but it was to prove effective, if not in the manner its author planned. Lord Blessington suffered a fatal seizure while riding in Paris on a hot day and Harriet married the Count d'Orsay when she was only fifteen years and four months of age, "a pale, slight girl brought direct from the schoolroom".

Victorian writers were prone ever after to hint at Lady Harriet's trials and tribulations without going into details. Even d'Orsay's biographer, Dr. Madden, rendered her only oblique justice, describing her three months after the marriage:

> Lady Harriet was exceedingly girlish-looking, pale and rather inanimate in expression, silent and reserved; there was no

appearance of familiarity with any one around her; no air or look of womanhood, no semblance of satisfaction… She seldom or ever spoke, she was little noticed, she was looked on as a mere schoolgirl. I think her feelings were crushed, repressed, and her emotions driven inwards by the sense of slight and indifference, and by the strangeness and coldness of everything around her…

What precisely happened to Lady Harriet? The answer is that nothing happened. The marriage was never consummated. Nor was her virginity due, on her husband's part, to any tender respect for her innocent youth.

Victorian society was outraged because the Count and Countess d'Orsay and Lady Blessington formed a *menage a trois*. The asexual Count "with floods of dark auburn hair, with a beauty, with an adornment unsurpassable on this planet" was probably engaged with neither lady. ("She was to me a mother! a dear, dear mother! a true loving mother" he said of Lady Blessington, crying with emotion, many years later.)

The journalistic insinuations were such that Lady Blessington threatened a libel action, but all three continued living at a house in Seamore Place until in her twentieth year, however, Harriet herself decided that the situation was untenable, and a deed of separation was arranged and she quit Seamore Place to return to her aunt in Dublin.

So heavy were d'Orsay's debts to tailors and furnishers that, like Lady Blessington, Harriet supplemented her income by writing novels, fashionably in French. *La Fontaine des Fées* and *L'Ombre du Bonheur* are two that sentiment may permit on the Sandringham bookshelves today. The silent, inanimate girl blossomed into "a person of remarkable beauty, *spirituelle* and intelligent," says Dr. Madden.

In Paris she met the Duke of Orleans, eldest son of Louis Philippe, and an affaire blazed into a liaison which lasted nearly a decade until a tragic road accident when he was flung from his phaeton and killed. In the bustling ever-changing world of the Second Empire she then met Spencer Cowper though it was not until after d'Orsay's death that they were free to wed.

V

Spencer Cowper brought his wife home to Sandringham in the golden autumn of 1852, when she was already pregnant, filling the house with flowers and friends and pleasure. Harriet's sister, Emily, was there and perhaps the Dublin aunt, Miss Gardiner, eager and smiling faces to crane around the cot when the baby arrived.

A winter of prolonged rain followed, and Cowper commissioned the young architect Samuel Teulon to design a garden room which should be rich and colourful inside and out in all seasons, a romantic bower of beauty for his bride. The architect succeeded in pleasing his client, adding a few balustrades around the garden and his "elegant" entrance porch for full measure.

In the prosaic terms of house-keeping, however, all the fireplaces smoked and the trouble was partly cured by replacing the chimney-stacks with seven tall chimney-stacks in the Tudor style. A Victorian bay window, too, was flung out towards the garden, without regard to the Georgian line.

But Harriet must have been full of admiration for it all, as the nursemaids carried her baby in and out, and as the months pass we can perhaps see Harriet herself blithely leading her toddling child along the terrace, a noble little girl, as Mrs. Herbert Jones says, "upright and rosy, with a crown of bright curls". Harriet's happiness proved to be all too transient. She had been a magnet to tragedy all her life and, in September 1854, the proud parents chanced to be in Paris with their daughter when an outbreak of cholera occurred. The Cowpers moved at once to Dieppe, but their flight was already too late: their only child was a victim and died in the Dieppe hotel.

The mother, distraught, refused to part with the last evidence that her child had lived. The bed in which she had laid, every piece of furniture and every article in the hotel bedroom were purchased and brought back to Sandringham to be re-established in the nursery "as a chapelle ardente", we are told, "within whose walls the mother, day after day, spent some solitary hours".

All the melancholia of Harriet's youth revived and crushed and defeated her once more. Her husband apparently had to exercise all his tact and restraint to deter her from taking the veil. Mr. Teulon was once again requisitioned, this time to restore the crumbling parish church and enshrine a memorial tablet to little Marie Harriet just inside the door, while the woman who had once written frothy French novels presently devoted herself to writing commentaries on the Scriptures in French.

Meanwhile, Spencer Cowper seems to have persuaded her to take an interest in one or two local cottage families whose menfolk had fallen in the Crimean war. Inspired by this new devotion, she took two orphaned children under her wing, a move which led to the idea of establishing, in a roomy old farmhouse conveniently near the hall and church, an official orphanage. However, "some difficulties arose as to the after-provision required," says Mrs. Jones, and the scheme was altered.

Ultimately a small private orphanage was opened in July 1858, with seven young children, two taken from London workhouses, others qualifying by being born in Norfolk. With part of the farmhouse occupied by the village school, part by the orphans — who also attended the school every day — and their matron, it was charmingly chronicled that "regularly every morning Lady Harriet walked to the school at eleven o'clock, taught for an hour and then she and Mr. Cowper took the orphans for a stroll in the park until their dinner-time at one o'clock... Sometimes, during the summer months, these infants were taken down to the sea, to bathe and run about ... their little limbs like pink shells on the sand".

In London Lord Palmerston must have felt that his stepson nevertheless did not have much of a life, dragging the orphans about, in the dull company of a sorrowing and evangelical wife. Whenever possible, Spencer Cowper escaped to Paris, persuading Harriet to accompany him and, in December 1860, Palmerston opened his newspaper to discover a report of Harriet Cowper's death.

The obituary, as we know, turned out to be a false alarm. One is disinclined to suppose that Palmerston was responsible, and yet it was precisely what he wanted, the persuasive decoy enabling him to plant in royal minds the prospect of a deserted Sandringham that would be an ideal sanctuary for the Prince of Wales. The false alarm sprouted the seed that enabled Palmerston to carry on all the prolonged wiles of the negotiations with unhurried strength.

As we have seen, the Duchy of Cornwall had accumulated funds of £660,000 during the Prince's minority and Lord Palmerston adroitly skimmed away one-third of this by the timing and unerring precision of his bait. Spencer Cowper was assured a fresh foundation to his life and even Lady Harriet professed her satisfaction.

"The large sum of money obtained, and the high station of the purchaser, were great inducements," she wrote. "We have every reason to hope that the circumstances of the tenantry will be much improved, but I shall regret the Orphan Home, the church, the schools, and the kind good grateful people."

Two of her orphans found themselves astonishingly whisked to Paris to be brought up "with great care" in a lush new mansion on the Avenue Friedland. A house was also rented and established for twelve old French women where, according to Mrs. Jones, Harriet chose and arranged the furniture herself for them, "with the exception of the covering for their armchairs, the colour of which each inmate was to select for herself. The old ladies, like bees, had some instinct which invariably led them to choose green. The little wizened Parisians sunned their brown skins in the warm corners of the court where their house stood, long after the death of their benefactress in 1868."

As for Spencer Cowper, he married a large and congenial American lady in 1871 whose ruling passion was gambling and they spent the rest of their days flitting through the casinos of Europe without regard to expense.

4: RENOVATIONS

I

On September 1st 1862, the Prince of Wales and Mr. White, the royal solicitor and man of business, stayed overnight at the Globe in King's Lynn and early next morning they drove out to Sandringham.

The Prince was armed with a list of recommendations drawn up by the delightful old land-steward of Osborne: he had but to nod his head or give an opinion to effect sweeping changes. The proposed site for new stabling for some thirty horses and coach houses for fifteen vehicles, the requisite accommodation for the grooms, the proposal for a pretty villa for Sir William Knollys, the new Comptroller of the Prince's Household, which was to be built in the trees to the west of the church, and the scheme for the renovation of Sandringham Hall itself, where reception rooms were to be enlarged by flinging two into one: all the heady decisions were unhesitatingly taken and lodged with Mr. Beck.

This was Albert Edward's first recorded visit as the firm legal owner of Sandringham. Returning home from the Holy Land in time for his second sister's wedding, he had stepped into his dead father's shoes for a round of official duties and had then necessarily accompanied the widowed Queen to Balmoral. But there he besieged the head gardener with questions and besought him to come south and give his ideas and advice on the Sandringham gardens. Henceforth every minute detail of the estate was to loom large in his mind. It was barely a week before he proposed to Princess Alexandra of Denmark in the grotto at Laeken.

While England still rejoiced at the news of his engagement, he received the reassuring information that Mr. White had further visited Sandringham with Mr. Humbert, the architect. A married establishment obviously called for a larger house but Mr. Humbert fully understood what was required and would be submitting designs for a suitable new wing in Norfolk style.

The wedding to Princess Alexandra was set for March 10th and in the intervening months the round-faced little Prince was frequently at Sandringham, planning, inspecting, fretting over Mr. Humbert's new designs and imperiously harrying surveyors and builders with unquenchable energy.

As soon as frost hardened the ground, the first sporting trials were made against the pestilential rabbit population and other nuisances. "Fancy on Saturday last a reporter from Lynn actually joined the beaters while we were shooting," the Prince reported in one of his earliest Sandringham letters, "but as I very nearly shot him in the legs as a rabbit was passing, he very soon gave me a wide berth. Gen. Knollys then informed him that his presence was not required, and he skedaddled, as the Yankees call it. The next day he wrote an apology for his infamous conduct and I don't think he will trouble us any more."

But the rapid transformation scene at Sandringham — though nothing of what was to follow within ten years — widely aroused romantic interest and curiosity.

The armies of labourers who had toiled in the marshes on the Hunstanton railway were switched to the new roads across the Sandringham heights. Wagons rolled towards the estate from morning till night. Cottages disappeared, new lodges arose, new vistas were opened, as if the Prince, like a Grand Caliph, had merely to clap his hands.

To the south-east, at Appleton, a ramshackle farmhouse had long since been built in the ruins of the old Paston property. The ill-fitting doors of its nine separate entrances clattered in every wind, damp oozed through the brick floors and everything looked so suggestive of rheumatism that the tenants, Mr. and Mrs. Cresswell, lived on the upper floor.

Up the ladder of the staircase went the Prince to gaze around Mrs. Cresswell's parlour with an amused eye, to inspect the plan of a dream house that she and her husband had sketched for amusement and to promise that it should be put into effect at once. He was as good as his word, and the new work pleasantly paid due regard to the old nut walk, the nearby ruined church and ancestral vault, the sixteenth-century entrance gate and other Paston relics. He had indeed but to speak to be obeyed.

Within a few months an expenditure of £60,000 was released on the property, an outpouring nearer to £500,000 at today's purchasing values. Another £60,000 was withdrawn from the Duchy of Cornwall accumulations for "outfit", though the Prince still hesitated at the greater expense that might be required for a new wing to the south.

When the Princess of Wales first visited Sandringham with her husband for the Easter holiday of 1863, the smell of new paint and plaster filled the house. But the Princess could sit amid the new furniture in the pretty rococo drawing-room and carefully pore over her prayer-book with Dean Stanley, who had been invited to take the Easter service in the church, and discuss the differences between the English and Danish services of Communion. "So winning and graceful," the Dean thought her, "so fresh and full of life … more charming and beautiful even than I had expected."

Lord Granville, another guest, sent the Queen "great reports" of his stay there, and Lady Augusta Stanley, in waiting at Windsor, happily noted the arrival of a letter from the Prince of Wales to the Queen, "such a nice letter from Sandringham, so pleased with his own place!"

After being alternately feted in London and surfeited with gloom at Windsor Castle, Princess Alexandra also was so delighted with the fresh and simple rural atmosphere that she was dissuaded with difficulty from calling forthwith on her nearest neighbour as she might have done at home in Denmark.

It was reassuringly like Bernstorff, though wilder, the day passing with the same serene routine. Her young husband was early astir, eager to show the guests his new domain, including the progress at Park House, the new villa for General Knollys. The afternoon was devoted to walking or driving, exploring the unfamiliar countryside, perhaps as far afield as the developing watering place of Hunstanton, where everything was on a miniature scale, from the new railway station to the six or seven bathing machines on the beach.

At Hunstanton cliff, visitors were soon being shown the rock where, it was said, the Prince and Princess of Wales were in the habit of taking luncheon, a servant "laying the cloth on one of the rocks, while the future King of England sits on another, smoking his cigar."

Nearer neighbours learned that the "royals" were not extraordinary people but a nearly ordinary couple who wished to be on "nearly ordinary" terms with the local gentry. A "small dance" was early given in the Sandringham drawing-room to show the way they meant to continue.

With the first full house-party later that year in October, a trainload of guests and servants travelled down from London to alight two miles away at Wolferton Station, which was in use for the first time, and to find with dismay that a steady rain drenched the landscape as they drove up the hill.

The Sandringham damp seeped into old bones but the young people laughed at rheumatic hobblers and any complaints that reached the Queen at Osborne were impatiently brushed aside, "Good air is good air, whether there be occasional disturbance and deterioration of it from unusual rain and cold or draught and the Queen is a disbeliever in the effects of climate on healthy people."

Princess Alexandra's parents, Prince and Princess Christian of Denmark, were entertained that month, talking eagerly of their son who was about to become King of Greece and little suspecting that they themselves were about to be called to the Danish throne. Then there was Alexandra's sister, Dagmar, who would one day be Empress of Russia, and among others the Duke of St. Albans, delighted to see Teulon's conservatory and pore over Humbert's designs for the proposed new wing matching its brickwork.

The rector's nephew, young Mr. Moxon, was invited to dinner one night, and every detail of the exciting new neighbours presently rang around local breakfast tables … "the perfect ease and familiarity … the only State being that the guests and the household assemble in a separate room from the Royal Family, introductions to whom take place *after* dinner".

The Prince played whist with the Duke of St. Albans, Lord Granville and Mr. Fisher (the Prince's secretary). He asked Moxon if he objected to cards, "in which case there should be none". Moxon played a round game of cards called Chow Chow, "They played for fish at a penny the dozen, Princess Dagmar being very zealous at it. They talk English but often break into Danish. They like Sandringham very much indeed…"

For the afternoon walk, too, the entire party went over to Hall Farm, which had freshly come into occupation, the first of a string of such acquisitions eventually destined to round off the royal domain to eleven thousand acres. Then Mr. Jarvis, the mayor of Lynn, "had the honour of dining" one night, with the fruitful result that he became a local solicitor for the Prince. (It is of interest that the Prince later solicited Disraeli for the favour of knighthood for Jarvis, a request he twice repeated with such pertinacity that, after fifteen years, Sir Lewis Jarvis rose at last from the accolade.)

In a simple form, in fact, the house-party of 1863 was already stamped with the pattern that scarcely changed for a century. The Prince discovered, a possibility not foreseen by his parents, that he was comfortably able to reach Newmarket for the Cambridge Stakes. On November 9th, too, his twenty-second birthday was celebrated with a feast for every village child of the district, and the army of building and agricultural labourers sat down to a notable board with "roast beef, boiled beef, roast mutton, potatoes, plum pudding, cheese, apples, oranges, nuts, raisins and plenty of beer".

Another day the Prince drove to Snettisham, five miles to the north to take part in the fox-hunting with the West Norfolk hounds. The entire village was decorated and all the humanity of West Norfolk seemed to have poured to the spot and it was not until the afternoon that Reynard gave his followers a brief burst of thirty minutes before he was killed.

The Prince countered the Master's disappointment by telling him buoyantly that good sport was assured in his own coverts and the Hunt was thereupon invited to a meet at which they would be "less disturbed". They were indeed undisturbed even by the fox at Sandringham and to Albert Edward's dismay and chagrin his woods were drawn blank.

It is on record that in the severe winter of 1865 the hunt breakfast was served in the Sandringham dining-room and the run took place over Anmer, where fresh territory had also just been added to the royal estate.

The following year, when public interest in Sandringham was at its height, two hundred carriages and five hundred horsemen blocked the roads, with such crowds afoot that the sport was unrewarding. It was arranged that the hounds should meet elsewhere two days later. Although she "hoped the poor fox would get away" the Princess was also in the saddle, the young bloods so anxious to display in front of this beautiful woman that one accidentally rode full tilt at the Prince and hurled him from his horse.

The diaries of Sir Henry Keppel, a frequent guest, afford glimpses of this earlier sporting Sandringham and the quiet domesticity of the young married couple. "By 10.57 train from Shoreditch. Arrived at Dersingham 3.20; carriage to meet us. Prince most kind. Dinner, whist, loo, etc... Party here: Woodward, the librarian from Windsor; Frederick Leighton, artist, George Grey and Lady Morton in waiting; Miss Knollys, etc. Lord Hamilton."

The next day Admiral Keppel awoke to the birthday of the young Prince Albert Victor "one year old, fine little fellow". Then the afternoon walk was to see Brereton, an outlandish tenant of a smallholding on the estate whose eccentric habits and costume — unspecified as they are in Sandringham's recorded history — were always guaranteed to astonish and amuse.

The next day, January 9th 1865, the diarist noted "Prince and self planted first apple and pear trees in new kitchen garden.

Duchess of Cambridge arrived, attended by Lady Somerset and Purvis, also Lord Harris and Helps". And this is followed by the partridge beat the morning later, "some nine guns, with over thirty beaters to drive. The wind high, and birds fast for me. Great function was the hot luncheon in a barn. Sat next the Princess at dinner, most charming of all Princesses".

The flux of perpetually changing guests was nevertheless already not without its problems. There rarely seemed sufficient houseroom to offer hospitality as full and unfettered as the royal host and hostess desired.

A lone bachelor arriving with his man-servant — or with a man he had borrowed — required accommodation hardly less ample than a married couple with a man and two maids. Servants were inconveniently boarded out and early arrivals among the guests awkwardly clashed at times with late departures. Even the second addition to the nursery establishment (which proved to be Prince George, the future King George V) threatened to crowd the already cramped space.

The Prince of Wales toyed with the idea of a bachelor cottage to which separate gentlemen could be conveyed by a shuttle service of carriages if the weather disinclined them for a stroll across the park. Yet this could not solve the problem and early in 1865, after less than two years intermittent residence, the "Waleses" realised that the house they had bought and improved at fabulous expense was indeed far too small.

II

The Prince's instant solution in any architectural dilemma was always to send for Mr. Humbert. When an "improved residence" was required for Mr. Beck, the agent, the dapper, reserved Mr. Humbert produced the necessary plans as if out of a hat. When the Prince asserted that the head keeper's house should be Gothic, Mr. Humbert promptly sketched the prettiest of lodges with admirable bay-windows and projecting quoins and quite caught the Prince's idea by suggesting that the roof should have blue and red tiles. When the Rector concurred that a barn might become a new school, both a schoolhouse and a teacher's house adjoining sprang from Mr. Humbert's drawing board.

The Rectory and Park House, west of the church, and the head gardener's cottage in the east garden, which still remain among the most attractive buildings of the estate, all came as readily from his hand as a venison larder, a range of "miniature houses" for dog kennels, an octagonal game larder "supported by rustic fir-trees" and a semi-circular house for camelias.

Watching the realisation of his whims in solid brick and carstone, Albert Edward took his architect's willing versatility for granted. Albert Jenkins Humbert faced each new problem diligently, usually with good taste, and sedulously copied the idea of others when his own imagination faltered.

With his fastidious, autocratic and exacting royal client, he could however leave no detail to the contractor, a Swaffham builder, or the clerk of the works. Ultimately the piecemeal replacement of Sandringham Hall by Sandringham House was to take him a span beyond his powers, and one may surmise that the worry and overwork hastened his premature end, for he died when only fifty-five.

Born in 1822, of Swiss descent, his pertinacity was a strong family characteristic. His father, Lewis Humbert, rose to be chief clerk of military stores with the East India Company in London — affording us a curious link with the Motteuxs — and passed unscathed through the scandalous repercussions of the Indian Mutiny to preside over the government stores of the newly-constituted India Department.

Borne equally on the Victorian surge of self-help, Lewis's other son, Lewis Macnaughton Humbert, won distinction at Oxford University and within twelve years was the respected Master of the ancient Winchester hospice of St. Cross. Subsequently, he became rector of Chiddingfold and a Winchester rural dean, writing a four-volume history of St. Cross and surviving his brother by some twenty years.

Nothing is known of Albert Jenkins' education. Probably Humbert *père*, his activities centred on the India office in Cannon Row, effected an introduction to the Reeks family around the corner at the Receiving Office of the government Board of Works in Scotland Yard. Young men of the same age to within a year, Charles Reeks and Albert Jenkins Humbert commenced in architectural partnership together late in the 1840's, specialising in minor contracts with the Board of Works. This led in 1851 to the building on a stretch of reclaimed Crown foreshore at Hastings, of two stucco terraces (Carlisle Parade and Rochester Terrace) in a dignified style not far removed from the Nash and Italianate terraces of Brighton.

Attracting favourable local attention, as well as acquiring the Crown lease of a pleasant Carlisle Parade house for himself, Humbert was then asked, with Reeks, to undertake the restoration of the little Sussex church of Bodiam, a task they finished with such energetic thoroughness that little of the original fourteenth-century fabric remained in sight.

It has been said that Queen Victoria herself led the fashion for what now seems a disastrous passion for rebuilding ancient churches. At all events the Prince Consort next commissioned Humbert to rebuild and enlarge the chancel of the engaging parish church at Whippingham on the Isle of Wight, chiefly with the object of providing better seating for the royal couple when they attended Divine Service from Osborne House.

Nash had redesigned the interior some forty years earlier with theatrical side galleries supported on slender shafts of great elegance. Flattered and almost overcome by the attention of a royal client, Humbert eagerly carried out instructions and effected a chancel in Transitional style, oblivious to the discrepancies between the new work and the old.

The tinkering with Whippingham was to continue year in and year out until after the Prince Consort's death. Ultimately the Nash structure itself was totally demolished and Prince Albert started afresh in collaboration with Humbert, bent on a church to remind him of the Schloss Ehrenburg, his family home.

The resulting turreted and pinnacled edifice, Gothic and sugary, might indeed have looked better at Coburg. It was pure Albert, in a stupor in nostalgia, and unredeemed Humbert at his most obedient. In climbing ladders with the Prince, Albert Jenkins Humbert was second only to Thomas Cubitt, who clambered about so incessantly at Osborne.

The two Alberts were sharing the topmost scaffolding at Whippingham on the notable occasion when the rector's son, the future Lord Ernle, having darted into concealment with a catapult, could not resist the temptation of the tight royal plaid trousers, took aim and twice hit his target, to be rewarded with mystified royal yelps before being detected, cowering behind a gravestone.

Meanwhile, the partnership of Humbert and Reeks entered designs in the competition held in 1856 for the new Foreign Office and War Office in Whitehall, the contest that led to the famous Battle of Styles. Their entry was awarded a premium and Humbert had the satisfaction of seeing his drawings exhibited in Westminster Hall with those of Charles Barry and Gilbert Scott. Yet he was still professionally ill-qualified and it was only now that he received his diploma as an Associate of the Institute of British Architects, to be followed by his Fellowship three years later.

Though other contestants were placed more favourably, Humbert for months faced the tantalising promise that the lucrative contract might come his way or that, worse, he might be disqualified. Lord Palmerston felt that Scott's Gothic designs were unsuitable and should be passed over, and that a Palladian design by Sir James Pennethorne would sit better in the metropolis.

Complaints and a select commission of enquiry aroused a hornet's nest; Humbert's plans were a suitable compromise and it transpired in the evidence that the designs of Humbert and Reeks were on the selector's lists. Scott however did not readily give ground. He submitted three fresh sets of drawings and finally abandoned the Gothic design rather than "reward my professional opponents", as he admitted.

Humbert swallowed his disappointment but he had no sooner overcome this bitter pill that the death of the Duchess of Kent, the Queen's mother, brought him a minor compensation. Having proved his merit in royal eyes at Whippingham, he was asked to design her mausoleum at Frogmore, and he worked swiftly as any undertaker. (Reeks appears to have released him from partnership without ill-will and they remained firm and lifelong friends.) Set on a pleasant knoll containing the vault, the circular and domed pavilion, ringed by sixteen Ionic columns, turned out to be a charming essay in classicism.

"So airy, so grand and simple," the Queen reported with pleasure to her Uncle Leopold, barely five months after the funeral. "Affecting as it was, there was no anguish or bitterness of grief but a feeling of calm and repose." Her husband confirmed these words with his own opinion. "The mausoleum has become very beautiful and just what it should be, appropriate, pleasing, solemn, not doleful…"

Humbert had for once worked with a free hand. The same grace coupled with propriety was completely absent six months later when, in the wake of the nation's mourning, he began the oppressive task of designing the mausoleum of the Prince Consort himself.

At the Queen's direction this was carried out in association with Professor Ludwig Gruner, who had commenced his career as a scene painter before becoming the Prince Consort's artistic adviser, and although his prime concern was with the decoration, the resulting cruciform chapel is harsh, heavy and unlovely. Yet Humbert worked as before at unhesitant speed. The plans were approved in January, the foundation stone laid in March, and in December the remains of the Prince Consort were laid in the sarcophagus. (Forty years later, Queen Victoria was also to rest there, at her husband's side, and so we can fairly attribute to Humbert the last monument of the Victorian era.)

With these lugubrious tasks behind him, the architect was free for the fresh air of Norfolk. He never married, and he was now so sure of affluence that he moved from his father's villa in Pomeroy Street, Peckham, to a spacious house in Fitzroy Square. We can see him, reserved and dignified, a dapper man of forty, rattling between the Bloomsbury squares and Shoreditch Station, ready to plan a pheasantry or take measurements for the latest thatch-roofed rustic lodge.

In the autumn of 1862 Humbert contentedly spent many an hour in tranquillity at 27 Fitzroy Square, busy with pencil and watercolours on the design of a new wing which would stand alongside the old Sandringham Hall and the treasured Teulon conservatory.

The Prince of Wales had asked for a possible new wing in Norfolk style and Humbert gave him a design firmly based on Blickling Hall with its rose-red brick and capped Jacobean towers. But this was much too like and would not do. Undismayed, the architect produced a second study showing the then existing Sandringham Hall enlarged beyond all reason, and again Albert Edward demurred. The dilettante Prince of Wales was to prove a far more difficult and exacting client than his father.

The Prince evidently hoped at first that his family requirements could still be fitted within the old shell. When this was demonstrated to be impracticable, he insisted that Humbert should retain at least the chimney-stacks with which Teulon had embellished the Hall ten years earlier. To this Princess Alexandra added her own plea that her pretty little sitting-room should remain the same.

It was useless for Humbert or anyone else to point out that the chimneys were linked with the fireplaces, that the height of the hearths controlled the height of the floors and that the floor level in turn influenced the entire elevation. As the estate tenants were to discover, nothing angered the Prince more than opposition.

Humbert tactfully marshalled his most persuasive argument and pointed out that the use of old chimneys in a new building would be unsafe. Every domestic architect has to bear the cross of some absurdity which has become a client's fixed idea, and for some months the Sandringham chimney-stacks overshadowed every other consideration. Mr. Humbert probably spent sleepless nights awaiting a report from Mr.

Goggs, the builder, on the flues. Albert Edward, having learned to man the estate fire-engine, then apparently consulted his friend, Captain Shaw of the London Fire Brigade, who talked knowledgeably of fireproof doors and concrete floors.

Ultimately the Prince of Wales agreed that the chimneys could be replaced provided their outward appearance remained unaltered. But then Humbert submitted his designs for an entirely new mansion that overcame these difficulties and he evidently suffered the considerable shock of learning that His Royal Highness considered them unacceptable after all.

As Gilbert Scott had done in the Battle of the Styles, Humbert tried again. The servants' wing was approved but a long and mortifying delay ensued before the fresh drawings for the main residence won favour. A visitor in September 1865 found the site of the servants' wing staked out "contiguous to the east front ... the park growing very pretty, newly planted trees coming on rapidly, the farmhouse facing the Dersingham entrance front almost finished, ten model cottages finished".

The park wall had also been extended and handsomely gated, especially at the northern Dersingham entrance where the mammoth Norwich Gates — a wedding gift from the county — were placed. Designed by the interesting and erratic Thomas Jekyll of Norwich, with a sumptuous ironwork pattern of wreathed flowers and coiling plants, the gates — a showpiece of the Great Exhibition of 1862 — were winged with a semi-circle of attendant cast-iron palisade and set in what looked like a desert of open space. Years passed before the growing trees at last restored a balanced perspective. But the placing of this massive gift became the least of Humbert's worries.

Unwilling to discard his Teulon chimneys, the Prince was more easily separated from that architect's perverted Gothic entrance porch, chiefly because guests got wet while descending from their carriages and, annoyed by their discomfort, he readily accepted the idea of a porte cochère. This was however to have a room at least partly above it, reminiscent of the original, and the materials of the dismantled porch, with its plinths and curlicues, were to be carefully preserved and stored.

The proposed conversion of the Teulon conservatory into a billiard room, similarly, pleased the Prince so much that he asked for more. Why not the healthy recreation of an American bowling alley, to be placed alongside? Humbert immediately sketched out a suitable hall one hundred feet long, extending towards the south, with an exterior wall matching the pattern of Teuton's brickwork and an interior wall of concrete eighteen inches thick to deaden the noise of the skittles towards the house.

In November 1867, a building report showed that the new domestic arrangements at least were making headway. The kitchen, thirty feet long, twenty-three feet wide and nineteen feet high, was completed with its adjoining scullery; and the clerk of the works, Mr. Schofield, was to be seen in consultation with a man from Adams of London discussing the fitting of "every modern appliance".

Housed in an extension were the confectionery and pastry rooms, the kitchen maids' and footmen's rooms and at the end "a servant's hall of ample dimensions". Beyond again ran a string of further outbuildings comprising the laundry rooms, the brushing and boot-cleaning rooms and a pump room complete with its adjacent tank of three thousand gallons of water.

In secluded isolation up the slopes there also lay the new gasworks from which the Prince proposed to illuminate not only Sandringham House, Park House and the Bachelor Cottage but also standard lamps posted at suitable points to give light in the grounds.

The purlieus of his dream palace were in fact ready long before the palace itself. Altogether Humbert submitted ten or eleven sets of drawings, each incorporating some new suggestions or amendments, while the finished whole seemed no nearer. Only his interior design for the baronial entrance hall unexpectedly found immediate favour.

While the architect wrestled with plans and elevations, the old Sandringham Hall still stood, and the Princess's Danish visitors found its "small English bedrooms" crowded with guests and their children. The last Christmas in the old home occurred in 1866, the older guests concerned because the younger people stayed up till two o'clock.

The ladies passed the days on walks and drives, the men went shooting, the evenings were devoted to whist, except on Sunday when cards were prohibited and young and old joined in General Post, a form of blind man's buff. Charles Kingsley found himself clutching a lady's wrist and, fearing he had caught the Princess, he let go, "but when the kerchief was pulled off his eyes it was only Lady Spencer".

That evening Kingsley had just undressed when the Prince of Wales came to his room to ask him to witness his will and they had "an earnest touching talk". The atmosphere was one of benign and settled calm.

In January, however, Admiral Keppel reported continual rain and Princess Alexandra returned to Marlborough House agonised with rheumatism. After two months of pain the physicians admitted they could do little to help her; the

Princess was chloroformed when the spasms proved unendurable. Her surgeon, Sir James Paget, affirmed that rheumatism might be caused by dampness and that Sandringham Hall might be damp.

The Prince could not have been more dramatically convinced that complete rebuilding could be delayed no longer. He could brook no more postponements: he would never spend another night in the house. In high summer, Alexandra still wore a metal support on one knee and hobbled about on two sticks, happily not realising that she was lame for life. Albert Edward had no alternative but to summon Humbert and resignedly approve his latest, final building plans.

The following Christmas (1867) the Prince and Princess with their three children stayed at Park House, new-built, dry and with a dampcourse. They listened to the gales roaring and whistling down the chimneys but when the weather improved the Princess gamely began learning to ride side-saddle "in reverse" and they rode up to the gaunt, deserted Hall.

The Prince inspected the building progress of the kitchen quarters alongside, but found it less daunting to undertake a fresh expedition to choose a spot for a wildfowl pond in the Wolferton marshes. Sir William Knollys estimated the cost of works in hand at this time at £80,000 and in one form or another the expenditure was to continue for years. The custom had sprung up of spending the New Year at Holkham, where two thousand head of game, rabbits and pheasants alike, would be shot in a day and a three-ton surplus was often consigned to Leadenhall market. The Prince admired the great game room at Holkham Hall, where 1,300 birds could be hung, and he instructed that Sandringham should have one equally large. When he paid his Easter visit in April 1868, this capacious store had apparently become a reality, a vista of tiled walls and marble shelves awaiting the slaughtered piles. The final and closer region of the servants' wing was also found to be roofed, with the housekeeper's room, the housemaids' sitting-room, the butler's department, the linen room, coffee-room, the steward's dining-room no smaller than thirty feet by eighteen, all the infinite gradations of the household scale occupying the ground floor while above were "the dormitories for female servants" and in the basement lay the wine and beer cellars, the coal cellar and heating plant.

Nothing more remained but work on the mansion itself. The demolition picks ate into the empty fabric of Sandringham Hall, the masons' yards and construction hutments occupied a cleared space to the east, and when the Prince of Wales next visited the site the last acrid smell of destruction had given way to the tang of the fresh cement in the new foundations.

5: THE NEW HOUSE

I

The new Sandringham House took shape in 1869 and 1870. As builders, the Goggs brothers of Swaffham brought to it the skills they had acquired in erecting local corn exchanges and Methodist churches in the red brick and local stone of the district. As architects, Mr. Humbert had to bear in mind his client's concern with traditional chimneys and gables while producing an effect of space and splendour on a domestic scale.

On the eastern entrance front, where the plans were closest to his original idea, the effect is achieved with conspicuous and romantic success. Sandringham in its original eastern perspective is a house of seven gables (though an eighth was added later), a house with a Jacobean air, a unity of roseate brick and creamy stone foreshadowing the "Queen Anne" flavours of Norman Shaw.

To please the Prince — in other words, to please the client — the entrance portico far outshadowed the ornament and importance of any entrance porch that Sandringham had known before. With the western garden aspect, the architect is less successful. It is a Victorian Elizabethan elevation, uncomfortably burdened with bay windows and balustrades. It cannot be fairly held against Humbert if, with the passage of fifty years, the style came to smack of an Edwardian hotel and was to be decried for as long again.

The architect had failed to resolve all the irremediable problems of internal space. The two end wings, each with three gables, repeat the pattern of the entrance front. The pattern of the central block, broader than the two wings combined, is however broken by terraces of bay windows which echo — at the client's command — the incongruities that Spencer Cowper had imposed on the old Sandringham Hall.

The reminder of the old Sandringham pattern was, indeed, completely Albert Edward's wish, to retain some vestige of the past while sweeping all away, to eat his plain cake and yet have it almond-iced for his birthday.

And the Prince wanted the autocratic transformation, as proud house-owners are apt to do, in less time than it takes to lay brick and mortar, to nail joists home, to trowel the plaster. His Royal Highness was determined to enter his thirtieth year in his new home, a house of his very own. A bitter winter held up work and, alarmed at the prospect of indefinite delay he rushed down to the house in March 1870, to find it vibrating to the songs of the Italian plasterers. They were still whistling and singing there in April, when he escorted his Princess over the threshold.

The carved oak Elizabethan enrichments of the entrance hall lay about like so many stage pieces, though the reassuring man from Holland's, the furnishing people, promised that all would be ready by midsummer. Moulds were still propped to the ceilings of the drawing-room and the Princess's boudoir upstairs.

The new house lay more to the east than the old and extended half as far again to the north. It was strange, walking through the eastern entrance door where once had been a grassy courtyard and, picking their way along the new garden terrace, the Prince and Princess experienced the oddity of walking in the open air where they had once been indoors. The conservatory had been in line with the house and in its new guise as billiard room, it now jutted perhaps twenty feet forward. The ghost of the old terrace ran through thin air, a few feet above a new range of geometrical flowerbeds.

The Prince expectantly came down from Balmoral in early September and poor Humbert faced an explosion of wrath. How could the rubble be cleared, the paint be dry, the parquet floors polished, the furnishings installed in time? Nothing seemed finished, except the newly-carved inscription high over the porch, "This house was built by Albert Edward and Alexandra his wife in the year of our Lord 1870", an assurance which itself seemed in doubt.

Darkly the Prince muttered that the labourers' dinner, customarily given in the coach house on his birthday, would not be held. But he relented when the day came and Sandringham House turned out to be miraculously habitable; and the men received a distribution of beef, beer, bread and cheese and the ingredients of plum-pudding to take home.

"The new house seems quite charming, a very great improvement on the old one, and nicely furnished. It is warm and very comfortable, and feels quite dry" noted old Uncle George of Cambridge.

The first of a series of house-warmings came with the county ball on December 9th. The neighbourhood revelled in a wonderment of anticipation. Never were so many gowns ordered from London by one small country district, even the impoverished widowed Mrs. Cresswell of Appleton going to the length of "routing out a trousseau gown that had hardly been worn and some old lace and sending them to London to be done up".

Lavish royal omnipotence had wrought a transformation in this remote region of Norfolk and the inaugural ball was the culmination of the conjuring trick. Instead of the dark heath and the soughing wind, the gas-lamps glimmered through the trees and carriages by the hundred filed up the drive to decant their eager occupants into the warm radiance of the house.

Instead of the torpid melancholy of the Cowpers: the flowing movement, the babble of conversation, the effulgence of the gas candelabra, the perfume, the flowers and fashions. Never, as the *Queen* magazine commented a trifle wryly, were such marvels of satins, silks, tulles and flowers.

The guests found that, unexpectedly, the hall was a vast reception-room and excitement momentarily dimmed to reverence when it was realised that the young couple receiving their guests were veritably the Prince and Princess of Wales.

Much-practised bows and curtseys were at last fulfilled. Coot and Tinney's musicians were ensconced in the "enriched gallery" of the entrance hall but open doors and the glitter of distant gas-globes beguiled the company towards the radiance and luxury of the drawing-rooms. And here formality vanished in admiration of the glistening chandeliers, the plate-glass mirrors, the white statuary, the bronze naiads so opulently bearing palm-fronds, and the "refinements and delicate colours" of the French plaster ceilings where plump cupids tumbled amid garlands and rosettes or sprawled towards wreathed medallions of painted flowers.

The ball began punctually by Sandringham time, and the clocks were kept half an hour fast even then, so that some of the three hundred guests were still arriving during the first quadrille. But Albert Edward adroitly left the dance to greet the latecomers, soothing the nervous with his extraordinary charm, encouraging the languid with his own air of pleasure, persuasively exerting himself everywhere to make everyone enjoy themselves fully.

It was a performance of gusto and urbanity, all the more extraordinary if contrasted with the melancholy of Windsor.

Recessions of domestic sorrow were still to come. But a mood of gaiety and brilliance was launched at the Sandringham house-warming that was to last forty years. It was, perhaps, the true flashpoint of the Edwardian era.

The Prince had considerately invited Spencer Cowper to see his changes and the old owner was staying in the new house. "I hope to meet you at the ball," Cowper wrote to old neighbours, and his host no doubt flattered him with echoes of the old Sandringham, so much still his although so much was changed.

The similarities of the ground plan needed no explanation. The old and the new alike had a spacious and welcoming entrance hall, and a splendid fireplace with iron dogs on which the logs blazed. The princely difference was that the new entrance hall had two fireplaces, one on either side, the second gleaming behind the three archways below the balcony, forming "a cosy corner", almost in Turkish style.

The new house repeated the long gallery of the old days, with a broad inner corridor — wide as any room — running north and south almost the length of the building. The embellishment lay in the cellars where a similarly wide passage extended, complete with a light tramway for the conveyance of fuel and other requisites: stopping at all stations, the Prince might jovially have claimed, indicating the modern new device of the hydraulic service lifts by which trays and baskets could be hauled to the apartments above.

The grand tour would have led Spencer Cowper to the dining-room, some twenty-one feet wide and forty-five feet long, sumptuous with panelling of walnut and marquetry, its centrepiece the rich expanse of walnut sideboard built into its own special nook opposite the lofty windows.

Beyond this the Prince could startle his guest with the billiard room, built as we have seen within Teulon's conservatory, and Mr. Cowper would have been startled still more in that day and age with the "wash handstand" built into a cabinet. One needed to wash one's hands after chalking a billiard cue. The Prince thought of everything. And then there was the gun-room, still according honour to a portrait of Mr. Motteux, and, most surprising of all, the bowling alley with its painted ceiling and frescoed walls.

The previous owner does not seem to have left his impressions in the Cowper papers at Broadlands, but we can suppose he was ushered through the continuous suite of boudoir (a smaller sitting-room), drawing-room (rich yet ungilded, fifty-five feet by twenty-one) and panelled breakfast-room (nineteen feet by twenty-one) to the small private rooms at the northern end: the Prince's workroom and library, which communicated in turn with the secretarial rooms overlooking the forecourt.

Probably Mr. Cowper was privileged to see the private apartments on the first floor: perhaps he was even proudly shown the Princess's bathroom, with its bath sunk out of a solid block of marble. Resting, as the specifications said, on a floor of slabs of the same material, this was a marvel indeed with its taps of German silver and its globe light set in a special recess. (It seems a marvel equally that Alexandra was not gassed in her bath.) The Prince's own bathroom and dressing-room were identical, except for the sybaritic distinction that the bathtub and marble accoutrements were jet-black.

Man to man, the Prince may have stressed that, to avoid the risk of water damaging the ceilings below, the marbles were bedded on slate: and this may have led to a review of the solidity and weight-bearing qualities of the structure: the floors of solid concrete supported on iron girders and joists.

Captain Shaw, chief of the Metropolitan Fire Brigade, had been down specially to check the fireproofing. The Prince still harboured rueful memories of the day, five years earlier, when he had returned to Marlborough House to see smoke issuing from near the nurseries occupied by his two baby boys. His second son, George, was indeed only a month old at the time.

The guard was called out and while the troops rushed for the fire-engine, the Prince manned the top-floor taps from which a procession of servants filled jugs and buckets. The hose being brought into play, the Prince and the Captain of the Guard began to rip up the loft floor with tomahawk hatchets. In the ensuing serio-comic scene H.R.H. nearly fell through the rafters, which were riddled with dry-rot. After this salutary experience, Sandringham was "as fireproof as science could make it" and although a fire broke out eventually, that is a later story.

From the nurseries on the top floor to the wine-cellars, with their space-saving metal racks, it is safe to assume that Spencer Cowper was indulged with an exceptional view of the house. In the grounds, too, he must have been astonished at the sweeping changes Albert Edward had made.

The melancholy lake below the terrace, for example, had totally disappeared to be replaced with flowery parterres and circling paths. The site had been filled with soil moved, wagon on wagon, in the course of levelling a wasteland, and to the south a more picturesque lake curved amidst new-planted trees, with all the requisites of a miniature cascade, artificial rockwork, a cavern and an Alpine garden. To the north, a garden glade was dominated by an enormous, blandly-smiling Chinese joss, and thereby, too, hung a tale.

II

The Chinese joss still sits alone in his northern glade, overlooking the family corner of the house, and might be permitted to stand alone in our narrative. We have already met Admiral Sir Henry Keppel, who was one of the earliest Sandringham guests and helped the Prince plant his first apple and pear trees. Though "the little Admiral" was considerably his senior, the Prince always held him in high regard and was instrumental in 1866 in procuring his command of the China and Japan station.

Influence does not always blush unseen and the golden idol — strictly, of hollow brass — was Harry Keppel's outsize housewarming gift. Found in Peking, it had been stealthily smuggled out "covered with matting", as the Admiral explained in his journal "for fear any devote Chinaman should take umbrage at a god being removed from the Celestial Empire. The mandarin who accompanied us was anxious to know if I should burn incense before it when I got home. I have no doubt he thought I was a convert to Buddhism."

Presenting no minor problem in weightlifting, the huge figure was brought home on the battleship *Rodney* and shipped to Lynn, safely reaching Sandringham by road in April 1870.

Flanked by two lions of Japanese granite, it has in fact already stood at Sandringham for at least half as long as it stood in China. The Prince decided after a while that it would look better beneath a canopy or pagoda built by the estate carpenters and then discovered its inscrutable secret.

In preparing the foundation, the image was laid on its back and a great jingling was heard. The interior of its capacious stomach proved to be stuffed with coins inserted through some cranny by the faithful. The finest specimens were long displayed in a showcase in the house. It was, then, a good-luck joss, as its inscription showed, "Respectfully made on a lucky day of the tenth month of the twenty-eighth year of His Majesty K'-ang-Hsi. (October or November 1690)". A legend of a malignant influence might otherwise have glibly and readily attached to the dark events that occurred a year after it first turned its inscrutable smile on the Norfolk scene.

"When the house is finished, death enters in." Four months after the house-warming, Princess Alexandra's sixth child, a son, was born at Sandringham but the baby, the first royal infant born within its walls, survived only twenty-four hours. Eight months later, in November, Albert Edward himself lay at death's door in his blue-and-white bedroom, the house charged with whispers, the nation waiting in suspense.

Visiting a shooting party in Yorkshire, the Prince and his groom, Charles Blegge, had both contracted typhoid. The news grew so disquieting that the Queen herself hurried unwillingly from Windsor to her son's bedside, "nervous and agitated at the thought of this sad journey, weak as I still am".

The Queen and her attendants were met at Wolferton "and a quarter hour's drive brought us to Sandringham. The route lay between commons and plantations of fir trees, rather wild-looking, flat, bleak country. The house, rather near the high road, a handsome quite newly built Elizabethan building, was only completed last autumn. Dear Alix and Alice met me at the door, the former looking thin and anxious, and with tears in her eyes, she took me at once through the great hall upstairs to my rooms, three in number.

"I took off my things and went over to Bertie's room and was allowed to step in from behind a screen and see him sleeping or dozing. The room was dark and only one lamp burning so that I could not see him well. He was lying rather flat on his back, breathing rather rapidly and loudly. Of course the watching is constant and dear Alix does a great deal herself. How all reminded me so vividly and sadly of my dearest Albert's illness. Went over to take tea in Alix's pretty room… Dined with Alix, Alice and Affie in a small room below. Afterwards we went upstairs and into Bertie's sitting-room."

Evidently reassured, the Queen returned home but the Prince shortly afterwards had a relapse and for the first time Sandringham passed under the anxious scrutiny of the world. The frightened servants in the upper corridor could hear the patient in delirium, wildly singing, whistling, talking in every kind of language.

Lord Granville informed the Queen that "there hardly seems to be hope left" and she once more rushed to Sandringham, this time to stay eleven days. On this occasion the whole Royal Family gathered, and finding house-room for so large a number, as the Queen's secretary wrote, "considering they were by no means all on good terms with one another, made the arrangements far from easy". Besides, everyone was frightened of Queen Victoria.

Henry Ponsonby recorded the occasion when, about to stroll in the garden, "we were suddenly nearly carried away by a stampede of royalties, headed by the Duke of Cambridge … going as fast as they could. We thought it was a mad bull. But they cried out 'The Queen, the Queen', and we all dashed into the house again and waited behind the door till the road was clear".

The risk of infection also secretly worried nearly everyone in the house, the Duke of Cambridge particularly insisting there was a bad smell in the library — "By George, I won't sit here!" — and fretting till the drains were examined. Next day a mild little man, dragged hither and thither by the Duke and Dr.

Jenner, finally discovered and rectified a leaking gas pipe not far from the patient's bedroom. Royal sickness had its lighter side.

And yet on December 11th, as many as five alarming bulletins were sent from the house by electric telegraph. The physicians went back and forth between the royal sickbed and that of the groom near the stables. The nation superstitiously awaited the dreadful 14th, the tenth anniversary of the Queen's great bereavement, only to find that the 8 a.m. bulletin spoke of some abatement of the symptoms, and with succeeding bulletins a great wave of rejoicing was evoked.

The Prince recovered and it was the groom who died. Instead of Gladstone's fear of an "irreparable calamnity", Blegge was buried in the churchyard and the Princess of Wales paid for his gravestone with its complacent text, "The one was taken, the other left".

III

Early in the New Year of 1872 the Princess of Wales was able to take her convalescent husband out in the pony-carriage, continually stopping to receive congratulations on the roads. On the eve of their ninth wedding anniversary, they set off for Italy as if for a second honeymoon, leaving Sandringham to the old tranquil routine, the lambing of the sheep that grazed the park, the Spring planting of flowerbeds that perhaps only local folk would see, the movement of the cattle towards the marshes, the purposeful, secret life that was always resumed whenever the Household returned to London.

Mr. Onslow, the rector, would be seen, calling upon Mrs. Cresswell; Mrs. Butler, the housekeeper, would consent to receive and was received by Mrs. Mackellar, the wife of the head gardener. These, too, were part of Sandringham, the families of the agent and the head keeper, the Becks and the Jacksons, old "Mr. C" at the Lodge and Mrs. Barker, the dairy-woman, the Princes-by-surname and Westovers at the stables and wily Pooley of Wolferton Creek, who knew every inch of the salt inlets, and supplied many a tea of shrimps to the servants' hall.

There was the village lunatic who prowled the woods and paddocks and one day had to leave his lodgings after attacking the family with a pitchfork. None wished to send the poor wretch to an asylum, so he next lived in a hidey-hole on the heath, where he might have remained but for stealing a housewife's saucepan, which delivered him into the arms of the law and so into the asylum at last.

Then there was the local ne'er-do-well and poacher, who ran up a shanty on a corner of the estate just sufficient to shelter his wife and children, upholding his free rights and stolidly refusing to live in a house although one was built for him at the Princess's express desire. There were the journeymen gardeners who earned their 16s. a week and the apprentices who lived at home for half that wage. It was to be another fifteen years before the Prince built a "bothy" to house thirty bachelor gardeners.

At the census of 1861 the population of Sandringham parish was fifty. In 1871 it had risen to eighty-one, but when a census chanced to coincide with a royal visit the figure was 191, and an extra two hundred workfolk had also moved into Wolferton, Dersingham and West Newton. In addition, there was Hakim, an attachment of the Royal Household who escaped the census-taker chiefly because none knew how to cope with the mystery of his full name, his age and antecedents.

Hakim aroused as much awe and suspicion at Sandringham as Mr. John Brown did at Balmoral, although the housekeeper would plead he was only a boy, and a heathen. He was the latter, at least, until he became baptised at Sandringham Church with the Prince and Princess attending in person as sponsors.

Hakim had, in reality, been royally kidnapped. When the "Waleses" were visiting Egypt, he had appeared at Wadi Haifa one night, watching the camp torches, "an intelligent, ugly little boy, with a large silver ring stuck in one ear". The Prince and Princess took a fancy to him and the boy knew how to pitch a tale to the foreigners. His father was dead, his mother remarried in Cairo, he had no friend in the world. The royal couple were moved to pity and instead of offering baksheesh, they whisked him back to Sandringham as a pipe-cleaner and coffee-boy.

Hakim originally had no possessions whatsoever save his little white linen shirt and his little white cap and the silver ring and his ideas of property were vague. This led to trouble when, in more gorgeous Oriental robes, made a fuss of, he stole a guest's umbrella or gloves and claimed with flashing smiles that they were gifts, or when he ordered a boxful of neckties at a shop and said that the bill should be sent to the Prince. The correction of religious instruction was applied, despairingly when Mrs. Butler one day questioned whether he knew the Eighth Commandment. Hakim gave his broadest smile, "Yes, ma'am. Thou shalt have no other gods but *me!*"

Or so it was said. When, finally, he illicitly abstracted his master's new gun from the gun-room and used it until he broke it, replacing it without saying a word, it was too much. Hakim was transferred to service with one of Mr. Onslow's friends and so disappeared from the Sandringham scene.

The lower servants were always changing. With wages such as 20s. with a bothy, coal and light for a garden foreman, the more superior were apt to grow grey and earn a medal in royal service. Except the apprentices, the Sandringham gardeners did not apparently have to make up time spent at the flower-show. The housemaids and footmen found nothing amiss in a ten-hour day and a sixty-hour week.

Romances often occurred between the visiting and resident staff, as when "Old C" of the Lodge married an ex-housekeeper from Buckingham Palace, and John Blackburn, Sandringham serjeant-footman, married Mary Wagland, the second nurse of Marlborough House, a ceremony that found the Prince and Princess and the children gaily sharing "opposite sides" in Sandringham Church. Then there were the outings and annual treats, culminating in the superlative caper of the servants' ball.

Our friend, Mrs. Cresswell, has fortunately left us a living picture:

One year the Marlborough House servants came down by special train, and the rival establishments were in great force, the decided belle of the evening being Madame Francatelli, who did not belong to the household but was invited out of compliment to the distinguished *chef*, and was most becomingly dressed, and not at all forward or flirtatious.

The ball opened with a country dance, the Prince and Princess leading off with the heads of the respective departments; and the Duchess of Teck with another of the upper servants. One year the Princess's coachman, the most diminutive man in the room, was her partner [she was a large woman] and the contrast was rather striking. The houseparty, equerries, ladies-in-waiting, and all invited from the neighbourhood. When ordered to join in, no shirking or sitting out allowed, and when the sides had been made up, the

Prince and Princess set off with their partners, round and round, down the middle and up again, the Prince the jolliest of the jolly, the life of the party ... his own Master of Ceremonies, signalling and sending messages to the band, arranging every dance, and when to begin and when to leave off, noticing the smallest mistake in the figures, and putting people in their places.

In the 'Triumph', which is such an exhausting dance, he looked as if he could have gone on all night and into the middle of next week without stopping... It was a mercy to have a quadrille now and then for a little rest. The Marlborough House housekeeper, who was attired in a pea-green silk, danced it in the old polite style, holding up her gown in points, and dropping a little curtsey to her partner each time she came forward. Then a jig was started, and it was pretty to see the way the Princess danced it, while the state liveries of the footmen and green velvet of the gamekeepers and Highland costumes, mixed up with the scarlet coats of the country gentlemen, and the lovely toilettes and the merry tune, made a sight to be seen or heard. Almost before one dance was ended, the Prince started another: and suddenly the Scotch pipers would screech out, and the Prince would fold his arms and fling himself into a Highland fling, and so on fast and furious until far into the small hours of the morning.

IV

The drawing-room of Sandringham House is dominated by a full-length portrait of Queen Alexandra depicting her in the romantic Medici costume worn at a ball. The artist, Edward Hughes, has caught the sad, inquiring expression of the deaf rather than the air of playful archness with which she habitually camouflaged her disability and the painting is framed within the plaster mouldings of the chimneypiece as if in lasting tribute to her as châtelaine.

The new mansion was after all built for Alexandra, and willed to her for life when King Edward VII died, and there she spent her happiest days as well as some of her saddest. She filled the house, year on year, with her gifts and souvenirs, her letters and pictures, until it was overflowing.

Season by season, exploring every local byway, she made the open sea-blown countryside her own. She became a familiar figure on the grass-verged roads, driving her little blue pony-cart, usually with Charlotte Knollys — sister of Francis Knollys, the Prince's secretary — beside her.

The Princess knew every corner and every cottage and always showed herself surprisingly well-acquainted with the affairs of the inhabitants; every scrap of local gossip was obviously shouted into her ears in private hours by the invaluable Miss Knollys, who became her constant and lifelong companion.

The Princess had but to hear of sickness to send a basket of linen-wrapped delicacies by the handsome Mr. Neilson, her Danish page. An expectant mother would receive baby clothes through Miss Knollys; a widow would be visited unflinchingly to receive the personal comfort of royal solicitude. An old carrier woman was seen trudging along the road to Wolferton carrying a heavy load of packages and was thereupon sent a trim little donkey-cart.

It has been said that the Princess of Wales ran Sandringham like a welfare state, with its cottage hospital, its village clubrooms, its technical school where boys might be taught carpentry and cabinet-making and other trades. The role of Lady Bountiful was a natural one and, during the fuss and formality of London, the tranquil comparative simplicity of Sandringham was never far from her thoughts.

The Sandringham sojourn commonly began at the end of October, probably because of the impression that East Anglia was drier in autumn, and lasted — with frequent return visits to London and journeys elsewhere — into January or later.

Albert Edward was always there for his birthday on November 9th and his wife's birthday on December 1st, no matter what visits were due to the Suffields at Gunton Hall, the Leicesters at Holkham, the Ripons at Studley, the Hastings at Melton Constable, the Duke of Devonshire's shoot at Chatsworth and other "regulars" of the social round.

An old schedule indicates the remarkable commuting possible to the Prince in a railway age. "January 1st. Left Sandringham for Wrotham Hall. 6th, Returned to Sandringham. 12th, In London from Sandringham. 13th, To Newmarket. 16th, London, 17th, Returned to Sandringham. 26th, Arrived in London. 28th, Returned to Sandringham. 31st, London. February 5th, Sandringham. 11th, To London…"

In March the Prince and Princess would again be found at Sandringham for Easter, and visits in July and September were not uncommon. When the Prince wandered off, the Princess did not always accompany her husband. Sandringham enclosed her, with its placid routine, its pleasant walks and drives: she loved especially to drive at frantic speed with her four Hungarian ponies.

A sporting Somerset parson, the Rev. John Russell, was charmed by seeing the two young Princes following their mother around the stables, begging pieces of carrot to feed their favourite horses.

Admiral Keppel returned from the East to be delighted by the spectacle of the infant Princesses romping around their parents. An absurd story survives that Alexandra had but to clap her hands to have her babies lowered from the nursery through a hole in the ceiling and possibly the legend originated in some private family joke about the service lift. The jokes were constant. Disraeli at dinner with thirty Sandringham guests felt tiny fingers pinching his legs and found that a little Princess had been mischievously sent under the table for that express purpose.

Chronicled ad nauseum, as they have been, the record of Albert Edward's infidelities has been allowed to detract unduly from his kindness and tenderness as a father and husband, the more amiable qualities he always displayed at Sandringham. The storm of the Mordaunt divorce case, in which the Prince had been compelled to give evidence, receded with the dark clouds of his illness and the clearer skies ushered in the halcyon years of the Princess's marriage.

Disraeli whose discerning eyes were not readily deceived noticed the new atmosphere of marital happiness, the "charming children whom he is constantly embracing, and a wife whom he really loves". Sandringham, too, was the great enslaver. "He is really fond of this place, is making endless improvements in his grounds… Then we are building cottages on a new plan which I should think was our own, for we are very fond of it; and we have prize beasts and patent sheep and all that sort of thing… We had to go over 14 acres of *jardin potager*, and visit royal farms and dairies. The glass houses are striking; one of them containing a grove of banana trees weighed down with clustering fruit, remarkable; and a parrot house of the Princess's with great variety of birds of that species, noisy but amusing…"

On the eve of what seemed a hazardous journey to India in 1875, the Prince could not leave, Disraeli thought, without a pang "not realised before".

The Princess was left alone, with the two tame doves that came to her hand, with her dogs — sometimes as many as ten to scamper around her as she walked — and was occupied with series of intensive family visits, old Danish friends, her parents (the King and Queen of Denmark) and her younger sister Thyra. But the Prince of Wales safely returned after nine months' absence, bringing with him aboard the *Serapis* such a cargo of lavish gifts and curios and animals that Sandringham was never the same again.

The children were jubilantly given a miniature Indian pony, Nawab, so small and so fleet-footed that he could be ridden upstairs to the Princess's sitting-room. Then there was a Himalayan bear, as well as an aviary of some ninety birds, a family of monkeys and other pets.

This was the beginning of the Sandringham menagerie and aviary and the bear-pit, which soon joined the "crane near the kennels", the dogs, the hawk and the hens and chickens as objects of perennial youthful Sandringham interest. For a time, it is said, there was even a Sandringham elephant. Princess Alexandra took them all to her heart. She limited only the number of carved ivory tusks which were distributed through the hall and corridors, because she disliked to think of the pain that might have been caused in their procurement.

She had tamed some of the wildfowl to eat from her hand and was furious when one of her recognisable "pets" was shot by the sportsmen. On shooting days, the Princess merrily maintained her duties as hostess in the luncheon tent but the sight of the feathered heap of dead birds nearby secretly moved her to pity.

V

Sandringham had enjoyed mild celebrity as a sporting estate for at least eighty years before Albert Edward became landlord, but he devoted himself with enthusiasm to improving or, rather, increasing the shooting, and his orders were so ruthlessly and systematically carried out that ultimately some twenty-eight thousand birds were slaughtered annually.

This equivocal gentlemanly preoccupation with the abattoir aroused hostile criticism then as now. In his passionate addiction to the new battue system of driven game the Prince merely followed fashion; he was bent chiefly on providing limitless sporting facilities for his friends. He did not wish to be faulted by such enthusiasts as Lord Londesborough who was heard when out shooting to say, "Oh God, You know how much I like shooting. Why won't You allow me to hit Your partridges?" Yet the Prince's forceful methods as the ground landlord sometimes provoked the resentment of local farmers.

Gridiron strips were cut across arable fields and planted for game shelters without a "by your leave" to tenants. Instead of the one keeper and a few casual helpers of the old days, a newly-imported head keeper parcelled out the farms like policemen's beats, and cottages for the under-keepers had priority over the housing needs of farm labourers. Besides, the new head keeper was to all accounts a surly devil, unwilling to exchange a nod with a local, treating every tenant as if he were a poacher.

"They're always a-spying here and a-prying there, and a-watching everything I do," one farmer complained. From the farmer's viewpoint, too, shooting day resembled a full-scale military invasion.

The day was ushered in by a procession of boys with blue and pink flags, and a band of gamekeepers in green velveteen and gold-banded bowler hats marched behind the head keeper, who was mounted and carried a silver horn with a sling of red braid. These were then followed by an army of beaters in smocks and hats bound with royal red and a trail of onlookers swarming regardless of crops and gates in a carelessly destructive spirit of high carnival.

The royal party arrived in a string of wagonettes and ranged themselves behind fences and shelters, each sportsman with two loaders in attendance. The head keeper's horn would signal the boys and beaters to commence their approach until the partridges burst in a cloud over the fences. Some became wily enough to recognise the sanctuary of the flags and veer out of range, but there remained plenty for all. After the fusillades, a retirement to another fence, the comfortable wait with campstools and cigars, again the birds, the firing, another withdrawal and so until luncheon in the marquee with the ladies.

The sport involved neither danger nor fatigue. A pheasant battue usually brought the greater bags, the birds hand-reared in coops being turned out half-tame to face the guns. The hares, too, were protected, feasting upon the crops and the Prince did not get to know of the bills, "for damages" presented by tenants, that were whittled down by the agent to avoid diminishing nett rent receipts.

The farmers groused that the more one had cause for complaint, the less one would get, and resentment deepened behind the sporting days. The string of incessant squabbles came to a head when it was alleged that Mrs. Cresswell of Appleton Farm had killed seventy-one pheasants in the plantations as an act of revenge, and the gossip was carried to credulous royal ears.

The indignant Mrs. Cresswell demanded that the Prince's Comptroller, General Knollys, should put her on trial and the atmosphere grew so stormy an inquiry was in fact held in the Prince's presence with no less than the Lord-Lieutenant of the County as cross-examiner and umpire.

Mrs. Cresswell was vindicated and the hearing cleared the air. The head keeper was transferred to Windsor and Head Keeper Jackson came on a quieter scene. Unhappily country grudges are apt to disappear underground, and reappear when least expected, like country drainage. In 1874 the Prince's eldest son, then ten years old, fell ill with typhoid. The fouling of water-springs in a wood not far from Appleton was suspected, and Mr. Beck triumphantly rushed to crow over Mrs. Cresswell. "Prince Albert Victor has typhoid," he announced, "and it's all your doing!"

The charge deeply rankled. On quitting Appleton some years later, Mrs. Cresswell could not resist reciting her grievances in a book *Eighteen Years on the Sandringham Estate*. Although one chapter was suppressed by the printer, sufficient was said to cause the Prince deep offence. Peremptory orders were given for every available copy to be bought up and destroyed. Mrs. Cresswell long continued to threaten that she would publish a private and confidential edition. But her own son had accidentally received a severe gunshot wound during a shoot; she had endured a great deal. The Prince could make allowances, but with Mrs. Cresswell's departure for Texas he must have felt that a virulent thorn had been removed from his side.

6: THE GUEST WING

I

The hospitality of Sandringham glows in the memoirs of the later Victorian era. The guest-lists discernibly develop from family gatherings and the entertainment of close friends and local folk to the great house-parties of statesmen and diplomats, financiers and politicians, artists and their aristocratic patrons, all that brilliant new society of which Albert Edward was the born catalyst.

Fortunately for us, the ladies and gentlemen were always scribbling. The ladies especially would assemble in the hall, the saloon, after breakfast, reading the newspapers and writing letters. The rain might be pouring down beyond the windows, the draughts trifling airily with the bobbins of the window-blinds but the busy pens were catching the golden light of Edwardian society and preserving the affectionate banter and chatter, the elegant leisure, the incessant pursuit of variety, novelty and distraction, the sugared life which was nevertheless not without an underlying sense of purpose.

The weekend parsons give us some of the early pictures of intimate domesticity. There is Bishop Magee, later an Archbishop of York, rising at 4 a.m. to face the vicissitudes of a journey from Cheshire to Sandringham, travelling through the day and arriving "just as they were all at tea in the entrance hall and had to walk in all seedy and dishevelled from my journey, and sit down beside the Princess of Wales, with Disraeli on the other side, and sundry lords and ladies round the table".

There is Bishop Wilberforce, experiencing "a good deal of talk" both in garden and drawing-room... "we chatted on till near 12. At about 12 the smokers all went to smoking-room, billiards and bowls and as I told the Prince I always went off at 12 on Saturday night I was excused."

Made of sterner stuff, the Reverend Jack Russell, the Somerset sporting parson, watches the dancing "kept up with unflagging gaiety till 4 a.m." before he sets out for Lynn in a post-chaise and catches the first train to London. A noted "character", Jack Russell so amuses the Prince that he is invited the following year and, absent-mindedly sending up his plate for a second helping of fish, he confesses that he is very fond of fish — and henceforth always finds himself served a second time. Offered port half-a-century old, it seems he prefers it to Bordeaux and accordingly always finds an 1820 vintage at his elbow.

Paying a second visit, Bishop Magee preaches comfortably on *And we know that all things work together for good* (26 minutes) and has time to drop a line to his wife, "We are all to lunch together in a few minutes, the children dining with us. We are a curious mixture. Two Jews, Sir Anthony Rothschild and his daughter; an ex-Jew, Disraeli; a Roman Catholic, Colonel Higgins, an Italian duchess who is an Englishwoman, and her daughter, brought up a Roman Catholic and now turning Protestant; a set of young lords and a bishop. The Jewess came to church; so did the half-Protestant young lady. Dizzy did the same and was profuse in his praises of my sermon." And yet again, Russell found "a house full of foreign grandees" and was not to know that they were mostly in-laws.

Then the ladies, changing their costumes six or seven times a day, would still find time for their letters and journals. Lady Constance Battersea discovers the young Princesses clinging about her like bees at the proposal that she should tell a fairy-story "Princess Maud climbing onto my lap", and fondly recollects years later "the five o'clock family tea-table round which we all sat, the Prince of Wales pouring out tea. Then I recall Her Royal Highness conducting me to my bedroom, lighting my candles, opening the wardrobe and looking at my newly unpacked garments, excusing herself most charmingly by saying that she always admired our toilettes".

The stout Duchess of Teck is found complaining at Easter that it has "rained without ceasing". The observant Walburga, Lady Paget, shares the common experience of arriving late just as "everybody had assembled at tea in the hall, into which one bursts from the outside air. The Prince was the first to greet me, the Princess was handing round the cups. All the children were there…" And later Walburga was unwillingly pressed into a lottery, "too childish to sit with three cards, of which one must win a prize". The days "were passed in walks and drives and the nights in playing poker".

Into this placid atmosphere Lady Paget nevertheless dropped a brick when she boldly announced she was writing her memoirs, "really comical how everybody was devoted to me from that moment, flattering me and making-up".

The hostess herself snatched up a pen, "We have had a good many people here this winter…" The flow was incessant, the cordiality unfailing, the pattern once established was steadily and faultlessly maintained. A quiet Sunday, between tea and dinner, would find the Princess at the piano singing "very sweetly a number of her favourite hymns". A discussion once occurred with "Dizzy" on whether it was true that nightingales fed on glow-worms. "We have a nightingale at Sandringham," said the Prince of Wales, smiling at his wife.

After dinner, the Prince often played whist, the Princess loo. The latter played for pennies, rarely able to fix her attention for long, but the Prince — when such play was possible — liked one pound points and five pounds on the rubber. A packet of £20 notes was once found on the floor. "Mine," said the Prince at once, "my winnings at whist!"

It was a rare occasion when the Princess enjoyed sixpenny baccarat because, as she said, a Chancellor of the Exchequer held the bank and she felt sure of being paid. Sunday cards were not prohibited and play often went on until it could be announced that "the sabbath being over, we may resort to the bowling alley".

Yawners would narrate, "the sitting-up-late here is dreadful. Last night it was two o'clock". This was late enough, for breakfast was served at ten o'clock by the Sandringham clocks and — until the insulating trees grew up — guests were liable to be disturbed by the distant baying of dogs in the kennels or the crowing of prize bantam cocks.

One glimpses the white-capped housemaids moving through the reception rooms with their feather dusters, the aproned porters carrying baskets of logs that had been hauled on the pulley from the cellar depths, and the ceremonious moment when Mr. Cross, the house steward, moved through the house to ensure that all was well. The servants perpetually changed the scene in the dining-room, moving out the ponderous long table in the early dawn and replacing it with small round tables for the quieter breakfast mood.

Except when the Prince led a shooting party, the royalties did not appear until midday. But a record of a breakfast tableau has come down from the nineties — a little ahead of our chronicle — "the men were in shooting get-up, and the ladies

117

in any dress they chose to affect, skirts and thick boots or elaborate day-gowns. No one cared or noticed".

Again, two tables were installed for luncheon, when the Prince presided over one group, the Princess at the other. Dinner was staged with still greater effect with the Prince's valet, Macdonald, tall, dark and handsome, posing in picturesque jäger costume behind his chair.

For nearly forty years the Sandringham routine scarcely altered. "Here is a house full of company... The word of command is, constant distraction," Disraeli wrote to Lady Chesterfield in 1875. Thirty years later, on boyhood visits, the Duke of Windsor found the great house blazing with lights "the huge hall filled with handsome people and humming with conversation ... in the adjoining drawing-room others would be playing bridge".

To return social obligations, two house-parties were often staged in a week, one running from Monday till Thursday, the other a Friday till Monday weekend, and year by year there was more to do and more to see. If shooting did not occupy the day, the Prince liked to propose an expedition after luncheon, usually to view the latest alteration or improvement, the newest-built cottage or his most recent purchase among local farms.

"We could look over the cottages together. I have made many improvements which I should like to show you," he wrote persuasively to his old Oxford friend, Dr. Acland. The eccentric Mr. Brereton died in 1874, enabling his croft to be replaced by a "Folly" in mixed Chinese-Swiss style, for which Mr. Beck conveniently produced a Scottish cousin as architect.

In 1875 another lake, complete with island, was made in the park, below the Bachelor's Cottage, under the guidance of a fee-earning specialist named Thomas, "a gentleman," said the

Prince, "not to be described as inexpensive". The following year a new pony stable was built, each door with the name of the occupant inscribed above in gold — Huffy and Bena and Merry Antics.

As well as the kennels, the aviary and the spectacular menagerie, there were always lesser wonders. A Sandringham letter survives, written by the eleven-year-old Prince George to Queen Victoria, "We went this morning to the farm to see some Brahman cows which dear Papa sent home from India and we fed them with biscuits and then we went to the dairy and saw some little pats of butter made."

Next, in 1877, the horrid doubt as to the contamination of domestic water supplies was dispelled by the building of a complete waterworks a mile from the house, with a pump capable of drawing seven thousand gallons an hour from deep in the chalk, and the Prince no doubt walked his guests to see this marvel. A local architect, Martin Ffolkes, designed the red-brick water tower — with an Italianate turret — which henceforth became a landmark for miles around.

"Sandringham improves in appearance every year," the Prince of Wales could write to his mother in 1878. She seems hardly to have cared less, but Queen Victoria duly expressed her view that the teenage boys should be kept apart "from the society of fashionable and fast people … you are constantly having. You must breakfast and lunch alone with the children and to this a room must be given up wherever you are".

The Prince knew it would be useless to reply. Yet, under his own parental eye, the boys were not permitted even the use of the bowling alley. They were safely in bed during the evening of impromptu charades when "the audience was in roars" watching the bachelor Duke of Connaught making love to Lady Paget in her guise as a shopgirl.

The illusion of the fast and fashionable hung willy-nilly about Sandringham. Even Mr. Gladstone, beguiled by royal luxury, abandoned his lifelong prejudice against smoking and blew cigarette smoke down his nose as he saw the Prince doing. Meantime the Princess had stolen upstairs to ensure that Mrs. Gladstone was comfortable and tuck her into bed, while Mrs. G's maid happily curtseyed in a trance of obeisance in a corner.

The royal consideration for guests, indeed was not only proverbial but true. A gouty squire would find a room prepared for him on the ground floor. A married couple who took the advanced view that separate bedrooms added spice to marital life duly found themselves in separate apartments. Even when Edward became King, he tried to check as host on the mischances of servants. One of the King's friends, Lord Redesdale, while writing behind a screen in his bedroom one day, watched the King quietly come in, test the temperature of the hot-water can with his hand and tiptoe away, as he thought, unobserved.

The three leading social events of the Sandringham year — the county ball, the farmers' and servants' balls — were implemented by "small dances". "The smart rich farmers" scrambled, we are told, to gain the hallmark of invitation to the county balls, but the house-party joined impartially in either.

Memories have come down of Sir Anthony Rothschild capering quite on a line of his own in a quadrille, of that sturdily-built huntsman, Mr. Villebois, "going down the middle" when he fell with a resounding crash, of the Prince noticing that his pretty partner was making mistakes in the Lancers and reprimanding her "in the most insinuating tones, 'I think we ought to have a dancing lesson'."

The winters of the early eighties often produced frosts of great severity which were made to serve the fairylike enchantment of the evening skating parties when the villagers had leave to line the banks and watch, "the lake and island illuminated with coloured lamps and torches, the skating chairs with glow-worm lights, and the skaters flitting past and disappearing in the darkness".

The Princess is remembered looking her most bewitching in a grey Siberian style of costume and cap, skating arm-in-arm with one of her ladies. She enjoyed thus disguising her disability of lameness; her favourite dancing partners knew how to lift her or spin her around on one foot, but she gleefully took the credit. Mrs. Gladstone commiserated with her over her stiff knee indoors one night, and the Princess promptly bounded upstairs two at a time and down again to demonstrate her agility.

II

In 1881 the insufficiency of the inner hall as a ballroom and the constantly lengthening guest list finally outgrew the Prince's powers of hospitality, and he determined to build a new ballroom and other entertainment rooms in a new extension to the south-east.

Probably the crucial turning-point of this decision was a visit from his twenty-one-year-old nephew, Prince Wilhelm of Prussia, the future Kaiser ... possibly the malignant animosity of the First World War sprang from the inadequacy of a Sandringham guest room.

The young German seemed to go out of his way to needle his uncle and Princess Alexandra could not resist putting in an ill-advised word about the German treatment of the Danish people in North Schleswig, a dangerous topic then much to the fore. Whether taking offence at this or at some fancied slight in the accommodation offered to one of his staff, Wilhelm at all events gave the order to pack and left the house without a word of explanation.

Albert Edward urbanely attributed his conduct to an "impulsive temperament", he could attach no blame to himself or his wife, but he could perhaps reflect that Sandringham itself was at fault. There remained an area to the left of the front door, where a new wing could well help to hide the stables and staff buildings.

The contretemps with Wilhelm occurred only two days before Albert Edward's fortieth birthday. The Prince seems to have felt he could afford to commemorate his anniversary by building on, but the invaluable Humbert was no more. Falling ill, and after staying for a time with his brother at Chiddingfold, he had gone to the Isle of Man to recuperate and died there on Christmas Eve, 1877. (He left only £16,000.) A new architect had to be found and the choice fell on Robert Edis, whom the Prince had perhaps first met through a Norfolk neighbour.

It has been said, as if in extenuation of his designs and his awkward floor plans, that Edis was not really an architect at all, but this is one of the innumerable legends that surround Sandringham.

Conversely, if critics complain that Sandringham looks like a railway hotel, this is curiously close to the truth, for Edis was also architect of the massive red-brick Great Central Hotel, which was attached to Marylebone Station in London and subsequently became the headquarters of the railway executive. Not only was Colonel Edis a qualified Fellow of the Royal Institute of British Architects but he later rose to become president of the Architectural Association.

In 1881, however, aged forty-two, he was specialising in the alteration and rebuilding of large country houses and, with an eye to metropolitan opportunities he had just published a book, *The Decoration and Furniture of Town Houses.*

With emancipated views stemming from William Morris, Edis advocated that the chimney-piece and overmantel should be the centrepiece of all living-rooms. He favoured niches and shelves which could give an opportunity for displaying blue-and-white china to match the decorative tiles of the fire-opening.

He saw this tasteful structure completed in light oak embellished with carving: he was the father, in fact, of the dizzy and crowded overmantels that were to burden many an Edwardian drawing-room. With this, moreover, Edis combined an advocacy of "health by furniture", to be induced by graceful appearance and simple lines, a theme on which he wrote a handbook.

Talking to his protégé, Albert Edward would also have discovered their shared interest in fireproofing. On this subject Edis also produced a lecture paper. And not ineffective in the mutual admiration of architect and client there was Edis's zest for big game hunting, particularly in pursuit of the buffalo in North America.

Having fathered five daughters, Edis found it curiously necessary to emphasise such masculine proclivities. In his early twenties, when groundless fears of a French invasion had set amateur soldiers marching and counter-marching, Edis had been a Bohemian founder member of the Artists' Rifles. In his eighties, though honoured by knighthood, he still flourished the irrelevant rank of Colonel. Having founded his fortune with Sandringham, it may be mentioned here that he later designed a number of London board-schools, as well as such prestige plums as the Constitutional Club and the library of the Inner Temple. But we are looking ahead.

In July 1883, Mr. Dalton, the tutor, was able to write to Prince George, then at sea, "The new ball-room is growing fast; red brick walls looking down the avenue. I'll send you a picture of it when it gets bigger." When Prince George returned home the following year, he found the new extension an accomplished fact.

One can describe it as Edwardian Elizabethan: an oriel window on the first floor served to link it to Humbert's work while — a minor Edis triumph — some of the original Teulon materials, after twelve years in store, provided much of the new entrance porch. With its great mullion windows and roof turret the block constituting the ballroom itself might have equally served as the library of the Inner Temple. But now the people of the locality could attend a ball without entering the main house.

Albert Edward's hospitality became tempered with caution as he grew older. Now strangers passed into a white-painted vestibule, enhanced by white busts of royalty, which led by double doors into a "tea-room" or direct to the ballroom itself.

A description is best culled from a contemporary guide. "The ballroom is 66 feet long 30 feet 6 inches wide and 23 feet high. The walls are lined to a height of six feet with a panelled dado, and from the enriched frieze and cornice springs a wagon-headed ceiling of white plaster, divided into ornamental panels. At the sides of the room are deep recessed alcoves. On the east are large bay windows, and other windows give light from the north. The fireplace is highly decorated, the grate being of iron and brass with elaborate mantel and other surroundings."

The arch apostle of overmantels had in fact gone to town on that fireplace though the wing was actually heated by the highly modern procedure of "passing cold exterior air over hot water pipes concealed in the window-seats".

With this ample apartment embellished with Indian shields and tiger-skins, camel drums and brilliant elephant cloths, with the gleaming oak parquet hidden by a happily waltzing throng, with the 126 dazzling gas-jets, spluttering their illumination at full strength, Albert Edward must have been happily convinced that, once again, his money was well spent. In addition, the provision of new apartments for the comptroller and equerries, of four extra bedrooms and extra rooms for the post-office freed useful guest accommodation in the main house.

These amenities were moreover amply ready in time for the Duke of Clarence's coming-of-age — as heir to the house and heir presumptive to the throne — in January 1885. The Prince and Princess of Wales had planned a day of elaborate surprises. When Prince "Eddy" had received his mountain of family gifts, when addresses and gifts had been presented by the tenantry and by the Corporations of Norwich and Lynn, he was led to the front door to discover probably the strangest scene that Sandringham ever witnessed.

First all the retainers, headed by Beck and Jackson, passed in procession and then, up the broad drive, along the leafless avenue of giant lime trees, came richly caparisoned elephants and camels, whooping wild west riders mounted on rearing horses, red-faced bandsmen and tumbling clowns. With deep conspiracy, Sanger's Circus had been diverted from a tour of Norfolk, the big tent was pitched in the grounds and two performances, one for the Household, another for the villagers and estate workers, filled the afternoon.

A ball was announced for the evening but this too contained its happy surprise, for instead of a cleared floor the six hundred guests found the ballroom filled with seating. Mysterious hammering, it was disclosed, had been devoted to the erection of a stage; and Toole, one of London's greatest comedians, appeared in a performance of one of his successful farces, the first of many Sandringham productions that were to involve every leading theatrical star of the day.

No doubt, too, it was a week of practical jokes, with the teenage Princesses, Louise, Victoria and Maud, giggling and plotting. The hoaxes and horseplay of Sandringham were to be wistfully remembered decades later — the bull's-eyes and other sticky sweets stuffed in the pockets of Uncle Affie's evening clothes, the buckets of water set to trap the unwary, the bogus telegrams, the soap innocently served as cheese.

Albert Edward, in his mid-forties, was not above stealing up the private staircase to prepare an apple-pie bed. One joker released Charlie, one of the bears, from his pit, perhaps intending that he should amble towards the house. The jest misfired and the gardeners spent the morning with sticks and nets rounding up the fugitive in the park. Next day a newspaper enquired what might have resulted if the bear "had happened upon a healthy young Norfolk nursemaid in charge of a plump and inviting baby".

Another exploit, talked of for years, was when Lord Charles Beresford doped a cockerel from the farm and thrust it with tied legs under the brass bedstead of a fellow guest. With the dawn, the drugged cockerel recovered and aroused half the house. One imagines that the 1820 port explains the Prince's exuberance when he emptied a bottle of brandy over Christopher Sykes or liberally sprinkled his friend's bed with a watering can.

Even the dour and brooding Mr. Gladstone was not altogether immune from such pranks. When he spent a weekend at Sandringham in 1883, the coming of Sunday, April 1st, proved irresistible. Prominent members of the Liberal party throughout the district received invitations to lunch with the Prime Minister at Sandringham. The hoax letters convincingly bore the Sandringham postmark — available to anyone who used a box in the grounds — and the Prince and the Premier returned from church to find the drive a confused mass of carriages, some still arriving while others were being turned away.

As it happened the Prince was already exploding with wrath for, during the church service the village grocer had grown so nervous and confused at the thought of playing for Gladstone that the organ had been mute during hymns and had squeaked during prayers. It was all most trying.

III

The house was often, needless to say, in far quieter family mood. The shutters of reminiscence open on two different occasions in 1887. The memoirs of Lady Randolph Churchill recall the elaborate tea-gowns of the early November evenings:

> Afterwards Signor Tosti, a great favourite, might be made to sing some of his charming songs, and would ramble on in his delightful impromptu manner for hours. Sometimes I played duets with the Princess, who was particularly fond of Brahms' Hungarian dances, or we would go to Princess Victoria's sitting-room, where there were two pianos, and struggle with a concerto of Schumann.

And then it is Christmas Day and Captain Stephenson, Admiral Keppel's nephew and Prince George's naval mentor, is writing to Prince George at sea. "I wish my dear Prince George a merry Xmas, writing from this dear old place and from his own little room. I arrived yesterday with Harry and Miss Julie Stonor, we three being the only guests I see no change in the house since I was here three years ago, with the exception of a conservatory built next the ball-room, which is a great improvement, and must be a great convenience as a supper room on those big ball nights…"

Prince George, the second son of the house, was also soon to be home for his parents' silver wedding. Although this was celebrated at Marlborough House, a corresponding tide of silver flooded into Sandringham that Easter, particularly into the Princess of Wales' dressing-room, already crowded with objects and souvenirs of all kinds.

"The dressing-table was so littered with miniatures and photographs of children and friends, besides every conceivable bibelot, that there was no room for brushes or toilet-things," we learn.

On a perch in the centre of the room, or out on the terrace on sunny days, was an old and ferocious white parrot which made disconcerting pecks at everyone within radius but would take sugar peaceably from his mistress's lips. The silver wedding gift from her children was a statuette of Viva, the Princess's favourite horse. This she decided to keep in London, because the original was at Sandringham and "her equal doesn't exist", but the Fabergé Easter eggs were intended for Sandringham, "because they are country" and they are there to this day.

Romance as well as rejoicing was in the air. Young Prince George wandered the gravelled garden paths with Julie Stoner, who became his first harmless girlfriend and lifelong confidante. Princess May of Teck (the future Queen Mary) came visiting, to take tea in the dairy and ride with great enjoyment — "we did go it fast" — behind the four Hungarian ponies driven by a Hungarian coachman.

Prince Eddy was engaged in diverse attractions and the eldest of the three Wales girls, Princess Louise, herself found it a matter of personal importance when the Earl of Fife, a man twenty years her senior, rented Castle Rising for the shooting. Louise was in fact his target, and the snuffly, plain and apathetic Princess his willing victim.

Some members of the family felt it strange that a future Princess Royal should "marry a subject" but Queen Victoria deemed it "a brilliant marriage … as he is immensely rich", and the interest of the betrothal had the extraordinary effect of bringing the Queen to Sandringham on a four-day social visit.

This notable event occurred in Easter Week, 1889, and the Sandringham clocks were put back to correct time in case the Queen should complain, as she had done eighteen years earlier, "It is a wicked lie!" The clocks merely observed the old Holkham custom of "sportsman's time" and were not, as some said, kept half-an-hour fast as a precaution against Alexandra's unpunctuality, but no risks could be taken to mar the occasion.

Queen Victoria's whole outlook had been brightened by the renaissance of her Jubilee and her son put himself out to make her technically private visit no less memorable. The suite of royal rooms at Wolferton Station blazed with flowers, the road to the Sandringham gates was decked with Venetian masts and three triumphal arches, the grass verges hidden by enthusiastic crowds.

"The station was very prettily decorated," the Queen noted. "The sun came out and all looked very bright. I got into Bertie's large landau, open, with four horses and postilions, and dear Alix insisted on sitting backwards with Louise in order that I might be better seen. Bertie and Eddie rode on either side."

The Queen noted carefully that she was preceded by the Hunt, sixty in number, forty in red coats. "Everything came back to my mind, as we drove in at the gates, and I again saw the house and stepped out and entered the hall. All was the same as at that terrible time" (the Prince's illness in 1871) "and yet all is different... Bertie and Alix took me upstairs to the well-known old rooms, which have been freshly done up. I had some tea in my room and rested. We dined at quarter to nine."

The gentlemen of the Hunt had marched past, the Norfolk Artillery had provided a Guard of Honour and the distant white tents of their camp in the park had a festive air. Nothing had been forgotten. Even the green parrot in the hall had improved his repertoire from "Am I not lovely?" to "Three cheers for the Queen!"

The next day the Queen planted a ceremonial oak in a place of honour immediately facing the house, and the Prince then whisked his mother away to see Castle Rising. In later years, incidentally, the oak was ringed by other trees planted by Queen Victoria's descendants. Not all of them flourished, the tree planted by Queen Ena of Spain being destroyed by storm in middle life.

To return, however, Queen Victoria passed the second day energetically touring the neighbourhood and a deputation of the tenantry presented a loyal address. On the final night, Henry Irving and Ellen Terry were smuggled into the house and on the stroke of ten the Queen was led to the ballroom to find it converted into a perfect theatre where an expectant audience of three hundred were already assembled. Gazing at the deep rose proscenium arch, twenty feet wide, the Queen could not know of the pains taken to paint special scenery to fit the miniature stage. To at least one member of the company "the room looked very beautiful, the white walls showing up the many stands of weapons and armour, greenery and flowers everywhere".

To the Queen "the stage was beautifully arranged, and with great scenic effects, and the pieces were splendidly mounted and with numbers of people taking part. I believe there were between sixty and seventy, as well as the orchestra". She was thrilled however by a production of *The Bells*, and although she considered Irving "a mannerist" he "acted wonderfully".

The trial scene from *The Merchant of Venice* followed, the only contretemps being narrowly averted immediately afterwards when the Queen expressed a wish to meet Miss Terry and Mr. Irving. For the one was just changing and Irving had begun the difficult time-wasting process of removing his Shylock make-up. Neither could appear before the Queen in costume or greasepaint and yet the Queen could not be kept waiting.

Ellen Terry flew down the corridor with her dresser running behind her to fasten the back of her frock. Before the Queen had finished complimenting her, Irving followed in immaculate dress. "He is very gentlemanlike," the Queen confided to her journal, "and she very pleasing and handsome." From this dated Queen Victoria's renewed interest in theatricals and *tableaux vivants*.

The Queen retired to bed at one o'clock, while Ellen Terry and Irving sat down to supper with their host and hostess. Next day the Queen recorded, not without formality, "We left Sandringham at half-past ten, having spent a very pleasant time under dear Bertie and Alix's hospitable roof, and I was greatly touched by all their kindness and affection".

The Queen's huge household staff, her silent Indians, her ladies and messengers, had however once again taxed Sandringham space to the utmost. Equerries had been compelled to dine with supporting actors in the conservatory, and Irving and Miss Terry could not be accommodated overnight and had to return to London on a special train at

2.30 a.m. The Prince of Wales toyed once more with the idea of enlarging Sandringham, perhaps with a new guest-wing built over the bowling alley.

IV

Whenever the Family was expected at Sandringham, fires were lighted throughout the house for a week beforehand. The month of October, 1891, was one of exceptional rain and storm; and the fires in anticipation of the Prince's birthday house-party were lighted earlier than usual to help "dry out the damp".

On the night of the 31st a spark perhaps leapt unobserved from one of the forty hearths, or flames may have silently smouldered through a crack in a flue to ignite a floor beam. The servants in their distant wing began the day unaware of danger. The smell of burning was pleasantly camouflaged by the breakfast bacon. At half-past seven, Emmerson, the letter-carrier, was making his usual Sunday way across the park when he noticed that the smoke, heavy among the trees in the autumn haze, was rising not from the chimneys but from the windows and eaves of the upper storey and he immediately rushed to Police-Constable Middleton and raised the alarm.

The fire-bell clanged across the park, just as Albert Edward had always planned. As in countless fire drills, men rode swiftly on horseback through West Newton and Dersingham but now the rehearsal was reality and they galloped through the village fiercely shouting, "Sandringham House is on fire! Sandringham House is on fire!"

Men dashed from Sabbath beds or from breakfast tables, women rushed from cottage doors and all streamed, excited and panting, towards the mansion, where the glow of fire already coloured a cloud of smoke.

Sir Dighton Probyn had hurled himself from Park House tucking his thick nightshirt into his knickerbockers. Mr. Westover, the head coachman, was already at work with the estate fire brigade and their inadequate manual pump; Mr. Mann, from the farm, had organised gangs of men in bucket-chains from the lake, while others were frantically carrying furniture, pictures and ornaments from the ground floor rooms on to the lawn, running in and out soaked in cascades of falling water, heedless of the acute peril of falling slates. Pugh, the phaeton boy, was there, with Mr. Dickie, of the hackney stud, and many more. A railway fire engine was being hauled to Wolferton by special train and the King's Lynn town brigade, with their dappled horses, came charging through the Norfolk lanes.

All was done that could be done, though the flames could meanwhile be seen for miles around. Sir Dighton immediately telegraphed to the Prince of Wales, who was spending the weekend in Essex, with Lord and Lady Brooke at Easton Lodge, and Albert Edward must have received the wire with mingled alarm and chagrin.

He loved a good fire and was now missing the most personal blaze of his life. His friend Lord Suffield's place, Gunton Hall, had nearly burned to the ground after a chimney fire. Suffield had talked for months of the shock of facing the hideous, gaping, blackened ruin. Yet with *savoir faire*, to set his immense self-discipline in a phrase of the time, Albert Edward did not dream of disrupting the smooth and certain progress of Brooke's weekend by taking his leave. He merely awaited the next message, and was grateful no doubt that his wife and the two younger girls were in Russia, for they would otherwise have certainly been in peril in the house.

The fire had, in fact, begun in "the girls" top floor bedrooms, their eyrie high over the garden. The flames had stolen from floorboards and carpets to catch at curtains and bed-hangings and then to devour bamboo tables and overstuffed chairs and albums and photographs and personal mementos with growing fury.

By 8.30, an hour after the discovery, the whole top floor was burning fiercely. The roof timbers had been permitted to show in the plasterwork of the rooms to give a rustic timbered effect, but now they quickened the progress of the fire, catching alight from end to end. Soon afterwards, as the firemen shouted warning and the workmen ran for safety, the roof collapsed with a terrible crash.

Not until an hour later were the flames brought under control. Water dripped through ceilings and oozed from the walls. An arch of roof timbers stood out seared and black; the acrid smell of scorched masonry filled the air. When Albert Edward hurried from Essex next day he could nevertheless congratulate himself that his fire precautions had been proved successful. The damage was much less than he had feared. Only one fireman had been slightly injured by falling debris. Formerly in use as a nursery suite, the second storey had been soundproofed by sawdust packed between the joists. This insulation had restricted the flames to the Princesses' suite on the garden front, within one wing and the attics above, and the concrete of the lower floors had similarly held the heat in check.

The structure of Sandringham House had been insured for £59,000, the contents for £68,400, but it was early estimated that less than £10,000 would readily cover repairs. Setting aside the havoc of the upper floors, the worst mess was in the dining-room, immediately below the fire, where soot and water had sadly ravaged Sandringham's greatest treasure, the Goya tapestries.

The boy King Alfonso of Spain had spent holidays in the house during his year of exile. Visiting Spain in 1876 Albert Edward had specially admired two or three of the Goya tapestries in the Escurial and the young King had handsomely promised that copies should be made for him. By some error the monarch's order was neglected. When he discovered that copies had never been started, he munificently sent the Prince of Wales the original pieces. But the smoke and soot stains could be removed, the tapestries revived.

Perhaps it was just as well that the Princess of Wales could not immediately view the scene for the damage to "the good things" though superficial, would have distressed her. By being carried from the drawing-room, where they were in no danger, out on to the lawn, the carpets had been drenched and soiled. Yet they could be cleaned, the furniture dried and polished, even the waterlogged walls might be aired and repainted in time for the Princess's return. The Prince, indeed, characteristically gave orders that it should be so. His birthday, he announced, would be spent at Sandringham as usual and before catching the late afternoon train for London he had the satisfaction of seeing the first of a hundred carpenters, painters and French polishers commencing work on the ravaged rooms.

That night the Prince nonchalantly occupied a box with his sons at the Gaiety Theatre, watching a different bonfire in *Joan of Arc*. The Princess demonstrated with equal composure, however, that even the news of the fire would not bring her hurrying home.

The Prince spent his fiftieth birthday with his two brothers, his sons, his married daughter and others, and his wife remained pointedly absent. Squire Bancroft and other noted actors came in a deputation to present a gold cigar box and to stay for luncheon.

Jovially afterwards, the Prince insisted on weighing his guests — as was now his habit — on the "esplanade" scales in the hall, noting the results in a book, delighted when he could proclaim a poundage worse than his own. But he wrote dolefully to a friend that day that it was no cause of congratulation to put the best years of life behind one. As Sir Sidney Lee said so uncomfortably in the official biography of King Edward VII, the Princess was led abroad by domestic considerations on what promised to be a long stay. The journey was, in fact, her final remonstrance to his infidelities.

It has been said that the Prince never permitted any shadow of disloyalty to cross the threshold of his own home, except to entertain Mrs. Keppel there. But he had not yet met Mrs. Keppel. The marital discords were on both sides. Historians may never be able to examine the circumstances of the Princess's own wifely reluctance, especially after her last baby, who lived but a day.

What immediately concerns us, more mundane and superficial, is that although the Princess enjoyed the everyday country life of Sandringham, questions of building, decoration and furnishing were always left entirely to the Prince. They were his affair. So Albert Edward did not wait to consult his wife when he called in Colonel Edis to renew the damaged upper floors and also rebuild to a new plan the entire western range of attics.

Hitherto only two rooms had been set within gables in the roof of the main building, one at either end, The centre of the roof space was ornamented by a grandiloquent plaque of the Prince of Wales' feathers, with which the Prince now felt he could dispense. A whole line of store rooms and staff bedrooms could be fitted with dormer windows in the new range of roofline, and simultaneously the Prince decided that whole new corridors of guest rooms could be built above the billiard room and bowling alley.

Apparently two extra floors were originally in prospect but Edis demurred at the possible strength of the old foundations. So the single storey of the bowling alley was increased to two, with a pleasant emphasis on the Dutch style of gables.

Above all, the Prince insisted that the fifty-year-old brickwork of Teulon should not be marred and indeed that it should be the dominant theme of the new building. The polychromatic pattern was accordingly repeated throughout, but an effect intended to diversity ten yards looked stranger when stretched to one hundred and fifty. Thus this adherence to the Teulon tradition disquiets visitors today, although it is an eccentricity not without charm.

V

The clocks of a country house may measure off the days and weeks, seasons, even years, with sedate beat and placid chime, reassuring the occupants that change is held at bay. The rooms darken imperceptibly as paint dulls and the ivy thickens, until suddenly the defences crack and the doors are open to intrusive change on all sides, and so it was at Sandringham.

After ten days of energetic repairs, tarpaulins still covered part of the roof when Prince George took to his bed with an illness diagnosed — after he was moved to Marlborough House — as typhoid fever. This hurriedly brought his mother home and the parents set aside their differences in shared anxiety. But events were moving implacably faster. On the day the invalid was pronounced out of danger, his brother, the Duke of Clarence, became engaged to Princess May of Teck (later Queen Mary). A month passed in festivity and it was already January 1892 before they were all at Sandringham again, the recuperating invalid, the betrothed couple, the Prince and Princess of Wales, the whole family and guests innumerable ready for the Duke of Clarence's birthday on the 9th.

They had all escaped from thick fog in London only to face severe chill at Sandringham. The lake was frozen, ice hockey was in progress and a shooting party dared the elements, but the house echoed with sneezes. On his birthday Prince Eddy came weakly down to look at his presents but felt so seedy that he retired to bed. His room overlooking the entrance front was so small that from his bed by the bay-window he could touch the mantelpiece with his hand, and when visiting the invalid, Prince George and Princess May were just able to stand inside the door and peer over the top of a screen.

As late as January 11th, after three days' illness, Prince Eddy talked back jocularly to his callers. There was no sense of danger. No one dreamed that the heir presumptive of the throne of England was on his deathbed. Yet January 13th found him wildly delirious, talking wildly of his regiment, while his parents watched horrified.

Soon after midnight his death struggles commenced and every near relative in the house was summoned. With doctors and nurses, there were presently seventeen people in the tiny bedroom. When Prince Eddy died, the Prince of Wales wept, the Princess sat silent and transfixed. "I have buried my happiness," she wrote after a few days.

The despairing mother fixed her mind on the possibility of burying her eldest son beside her youngest infant of a day in the Sandringham churchyard but this was denied her. A phase of deeper silence fell on the house as the cortège rolled away. It was months before the servants talked in more than whispers on entering the family part of the mansion. The building of the new wing at the farther end went on as planned, bringing a new bustle and clamour but some years elapsed before the house parties were resumed in the old style.

The family started shooting once more in November, Christmas again brought skating and Prince George recorded the new year of 1893 in his diary. "At 12 we drank the old year out in the Billiard Room. I trust this new year will be a brighter and happier one." Yet, three years later, Alexandra, her idiosyncrasies deepening, was still liable to take friends and relatives up the main staircase and along the sombre corridor to Eddy's room where everything remained untouched, his watch on the dressing-table, his clothes in the glass-fronted wardrobe.

The Empress Frederick of Germany described the death-chamber and, two years later, a member of the younger generation, Prince Nicholas of Greece, was led on the same mournful pilgrimage. "My aunt looked at the bed with an expression of deep grief and whispered, 'Here he died'. She placed some fresh flowers on the pillow and in silence we left…"

Happily, events could change gradually to a brighter trend. Prince George was created Duke of York and eventually proposed to Princess May and late in the evening of their wedding day on July 6th 1893, they arrived through clouds of dust, weary and travel-stained, for their honeymoon at the Bachelors' Cottage, now York Cottage, which the Prince of Wales had made over as a wedding gift to his son. The young Duke and Duchess were putting the past behind them but some of their elders had doubts. Noting that they would go to the cottage after the wedding, Queen Victoria could not refrain from adding, "which I regret and think rather unlucky and sad". But her premonitions were not to be justified.

7: THE COTTAGE AND THE CHILDREN

I

The newly-weds arrived to a smell of fresh paint and supper and came down to their first honeymoon breakfast at a new table set in the bay window of the dining-room, amid a tasteful array of glistening new Maple's furniture. The view was a strip of lawn leading down to the reedy "smaller lake" and its island. The young couple began their explorations to the sound of quacking ducks in an atmosphere of new wallpapers and carpets and even new mortar.

The Bachelors' Cottage had been thrown off by the architect Humbert as a trifle in gabled Victorian Gothic, slate-roofed and stone-walled, merely to provide a guest annexe to the main house. Twenty years of ivy had softened its main lines and the indefatigable Edis had been commissioned to redecorate and improve the place as a residence for the Yorks.

He achieved this chiefly by flinging out new windows in bays of new stone and roughcast, and fitting the interior with overmantled fireplaces and white-painted panelling. There are signs that Humbert intended it to seem a miniature edition of Sandringham House. When Edis finished his earlier alterations, it could boast slightly enlarged rooms and two extra bathrooms but little more.

Following his father's example, Prince George bought the new modern furniture without consulting his future wife: he was astonished and dismayed to learn that she had looked forward to choosing and buying everything herself. The rearranging she still could do and she moved the furniture around and rehung pictures in her first week of marriage.

"The cottage is very nice but very small. However, I think we can make it charming," she wrote to a friend. Her mother echoed the results in a letter four months later, "Charming, most cosy, comfortable," she apostrophised, "the perfection of an ideal cottage! but far too small."

Promptly taking this difficulty in hand, however, the forthright Princess May tactfully talked to the Princess of Wales about the desirability of adding on and won her agreement. But as if to spare Colonel Edis's feelings, the new work was assigned to one of the tribe of Becks, an architect practising in Norwich.

Curiously, the various additions of the Sandringham estate invariably became outmoded although always conscientiously carried out in the latest style and to the highest standard of the day. Princess May's addition — Queen Mary's as it was to be one day — was a three-storey wing in roughcast and pebbledash, with a facing of black mock Tudor beams and a wooden-railed balcony to embellish the upper floor. By way of linking this to the main house a small tower with an hexagonal slate turret appeared.

When the sunblinds were drawn in the summer and the canvas awnings afforded shade, when the inhabitants could call and chat from their balconies, the effect had colour and gaiety. York Cottage has been variously called a bijou residence, an ornate hutch, a glum little villa, a rabbit-warren of tiny rooms, but Princess May thought continually that it "looked very nice" and it remained the Norfolk home of the Yorks for over thirty years.

Long after the Duke came to the throne as King George V, the cottage was the home above all others where he felt most comfortable and at ease. Like his cousin, the Czar Nicholas II, he preferred small and plain rooms and his secretary found him miserable when he visited rich Chatsworth and was forced to spend a week amid the Gobelins tapestries and ornate carvings.

In her old age at Marlborough House in the 1950's, Queen Mary could reminiscence happily of her "dear old home", the al fresco meals served at a little summerhouse in the garden, the cosy evenings when the children would come from the schoolroom and sit around her, each on a little chair, to be read to or encouraged to talk or, if they were in fidgety mood, mustered around the lamp-lit table with an educational card game.

Archbishop Lang recalled that the young couple showed him over the little house "with a quite charming and almost naive keenness. It might have been a curate and his wife in their new house".

King George VI was of course born at York Cottage in the small hours of December 14th 1895, and all his younger brothers and his sister, the Princess Royal, were subsequently born there, though it is difficult to know where the doctors found space for the necessities of accouchement and nursing.

Mr. Beck's architectural addition at least enabled the dining-room to be transferred to the extension, thus creating a second sitting-room, and the new wing also held a billiard room, nursery rooms and extra bedrooms, one for a lady-in-waiting, another eventually for Mr. Hansell, the tutor, with guest-rooms sufficient for two or three "guns", as well as lodgement for Tatry, Princess May's old French maid and other servants.

The Duke of Windsor recalled that in infancy he slept with his younger brother and sister and a nursemaid in a room dignified by the title of "Night Nursery". A smaller room where at one time five children spent most of their playtime and had their meals together was called the "Day Nursery". Such names endowed the house with a fanciful grandeur that in reality was quite non-existent.

To the left of the entrance hall, for example, was the Library, where the head of the house spent his working hours. This had the oddity of being "papered" with the dark red cloth used at that time for the trousers of French army uniforms, and these mournful walls were topped in turn by sundry coloured prints. But the windows looked north and east and were further masked by dense laurel, a strange workroom for the heir to the throne and later for the King.

As he worked, the traffic on the stairs that wound up to the first and second floors could unavoidably be heard at his desk. But the staircase in turn was a means of ventilation that preserved him from the cooking smells from the basement kitchens. The master of the house had but to mount the stairs to reach his bedroom and dressing-room. The children's dark and unlovely rooms lay farther down the passage, supposedly soundproofed beyond a green baize swinging door. But the soundproofing was relative.

In her own shadowy cell the lady-in-waiting discovered she could hear every sound through the flooring, especially the footmen's conversation when they were cleaning the silver in the pantry beneath. One day, when their talk had been more careless than usual, she sent word that if they did not mind her overhearing their conversation, she had no objection.

Such was York Cottage in its enclosure of rhododendron and laurel, with its dejected laden pelican beside the lake and its pastoral view of the web-antlered Japanese deer in the park. The shift of life from the "Big House" to this miniature but overcrowded mansion gave the younger generation the relief they needed from the sad memories of the Duke of Clarence's room, where fading flowers stained the pillowcase.

In 1893 the honeymooners were interrupted after only thirteen days by a family party who came to tea, so that nine people, complete with cavorting dogs, crowded into the sitting-room. Fortunately some massive Scottish furniture had not arrived, but Princess Alexandra took disapproving note of her daughter-in-law's furniture arrangement.

On a subsequent visit, when the new mistress of the house was absent, she shifted everything around with the idea of giving more space. The Duke of York wrote reassuringly to his wife, "We can move it all back again in a minute…" only to find Princess May disinclined to temporise with Mama-in-law. Such a waste of time, she pouted, when it will have to be changed. The following year the Empress Frederick thought York Cottage "very small but most charmingly arranged" and boldly wrote to her daughter, Sophie of Greece, "you might take many a hint for your own house".

The Prince of Wales equally enjoyed his new visiting point, though taking it too much for granted that he could call with friends and relatives at all times. The Cottage provided a convenient "warm-up" after a visit to the kennels or stables or the technical school where his sister, the Empress Frederick, now found the village children "taught to make charming things in wood and ironwork and brass and copper".

The stud-farm especially increasingly engaged the Prince's interest. County Council (Isonomy–Lady Peggy), one of the first produce, won the Ham Stakes at Goodwood in 1891, but the Prince's personal misfortunes were curiously accompanied by an equal lack of racing luck until 1895 when Persimmon (St. Simon–Perdita II) first won at Ascot and Goodwood as a two-year-old.

The following season saw the triumphs of Persimmon's Derby, St. Leger and Jock Club Stakes. The Prince scooped £19,490 from these wins alone and told his friends that Persimmon was paying for the Sandringham gardens. Though awkwardly separated from the house on the eastern side of the main road, these were now being extended and improved beyond recognition. The further racing win of the Eclipse Stakes and the Ascot Gold Cup, yielding twelve thousand guineas, financed the immense chain of glasshouses known as the Persimmon range.

The Czar Nicholas, visiting Sandringham in the summer of 1894, was puzzled by the company his uncle kept and found the house-party "rather strange. Most of them were horse-dealers, among others a Baron Hirsch. Even Aunt Alix was seeing many of them for the first time". The interest of the occasion was however focussed on a great auction of fifty horses at the stud, and the Czar was never a good judge of men or affairs.

Although Baron Hirsch bought horses and was not to be outbid, he was also landowner of one of the largest estates in Austria, his pocket a bottomless pit of profits from railways in the Balkans and Turkey. He entertained lavishly and the Prince of Wales had been a guest at his shooting party in Hungary in 1891, shortly before the Sandringham fire, when 11,300 head of game, chiefly partridges, were bagged in five days. Again, in 1894, when the Prince enjoyed Baron Hirsch's hospitality for a month, the slaughter included 22,996 partridges and more than 11,000 hares.

The system that made such large bags possible was new to the Prince. An army of over two hundred beaters started the drive inwards from a circle of seven miles in circumference towards a shooting point of about sixty yards where six to eight guns were congregated. The Baron also reared on the *remise*, or shelter, plan. These ideas entirely enlarged Albert Edward's views on shooting and underlay the prodigal battues that henceforth characterised the hospitality of his own estate to the end of his life.

From the mid-nineties, indeed, Sandringham enjoyed a fresh phase of renaissance. The turning point might even be precisely traced to the night up at the "Big House", when the Duke of York bet the Princess of Pless that she would never dare to suggest dancing. No dancing feet had enjoyed the parquet floors since Eddy's death four years before. The Princess spoke up, Alexandra pursed her lips and frowned, but the Prince consented and all the younger people, delighted at their success, danced for three nights running.

II

The golden age of Sandringham magnificence, splendour amid simplicity, was one for which Albert Edward was responsible, right or wrong, in every detail. His protuberant eyes missed nothing. When his youngest daughter, Maud, married Prince Carl of Denmark (later King Haakon of Norway) he presented them with Appleton House as a wedding gift but not before he had personally supervised alterations and refurbishing so iconoclastic that the sixteenth-century Paston gateway and dovecot vanished forever.

The arrival of grandchildren at York Cottage aroused doubt about the adjacent bear-pit: the two bears, Charlie and Polly, growing unreliable in temper, were dreaded by their keeper when he had to wash them every day, and the Prince had them sent to the London Zoo. Now only a Lawson cypress marks the filled-in bear-pit. Similarly, a neighbour was invited always

147

to join the skating, but came once only. "You never came again!" the Prince rebuked her.

Estate workers knew that the slightest fault might not escape notice, and reprimand unfailingly followed. Making his rounds one Sunday afternoon, the Prince broke away from his ladies and gentlemen to challenge a stableman, "I did not see you at church this morning." In a congregation of about three hundred, the Prince had noted the absence of one of the humblest servants. "You should have gone," His Royal Highness pursued, "I always attend myself and I expect my people to do the same." What the stableman said under his breath can be imagined.

The Prince himself in fact always arrived at church half an hour late, after prayers, when the church bell was rung as a signal and he would tiptoe in, with his gentleman, as the Duke of Windsor has said, "looking as if he had been detained by matters of great moment". Piloting guests about the gardens he would pause to knock dead wood from shrubs and trees with his stick and then explain, "I always do this. It's the only way to get it done".

The Prince was prone to exaggeration. He felt it indispensable to his role as country landlord to attend the regular sales of his shire horses, shorthorn cattle and Southdown sheep at Wolferton and at dinner would gaily proclaim the high sums obtained. One June afternoon he swept his entire house-party to the Home Farm to watch the auction of fifty-four bulls, heifers and a Southdown flock. Mr. Thornton, the auctioneer, did his best under the eyes of his smart and unaccustomed audience but this was a moment of truth of which it could be said glibly that "the prices proved less satisfactory than usual".

The Prince's indelible recollection of his constantly changing assemblies of guests, on the other hand, was astonishing. Chatting to the Earl of Sandwich of a mutual friend who had been dead some years, the Prince remarked on the number of members of a certain house-party who were no more and casually began to run through the names, "Prince Eddy, the Duke and Duchess of Edinburgh, the Landgrave of Hesse, Vicomte and Vicomtess de Grefuhle, Comte. de St. Priest, Baron Holzhausen, Captain von Strahl, Creppy Vivian, Oscar Dickson, Lady Kingscote, Christopher Sykes..." The thick royal voice went on. Looking up his diary for confirmation, the Earl was startled to find that the Prince was accurate and yet the house-party had occurred nearly twenty years earlier.

Towards the close of the century, the Prince usually paid an extra visit to Sandringham in June to enable him to enjoy the garden and his grandchildren, and there would be yet another series of invitations to crowd the extensively populated recesses of his mind. "My Time is in Thy hands," the inscription of the wall sundial on the guest wing constantly reminded him. "Let others tell of storms and showers, I'll only count your sunny hours."

Princess Alexandra had a beach bungalow at Sheringham, complete in its elegance to the silver dolphin of the doorknocker. Here the York babies were taken to paddle and shrimp and to help repair and renew a summerhouse of seashells which her own children had built long before.

The new rose garden, with its plashing fountain and scented air, also became the target of the traditional Sunday stroll. In the vicinity guests were expected to admire a sundial made from a fragment of old Kew Bridge and an ancient Greek bath, sent from the Island of Rhodes by brother "Affie" (the Duke of Edinburgh). This however turned out to be a consecrated ninth century Christian font when someone translated the inscription around the rim, and it was hurriedly transferred to the churchyard.

Young people might also stray into a maze of box and yew hedges, their raillery and laughter rising against the birdsong and the recurrent distant hubbub from the kennels. Deafening at close quarters, the barking frenzy was a sound the Princess could hear and enjoy. Her visits to the kennels were so regular that the dogs disdained to take cubes of bread from any hand but her own. "My dogs won't ever eat plain bread," said one visitor. "Then they haven't been properly brought up," was the Princess's teasing reply.

At various times Borzois and Russian wolfhounds — gifts from the Czar — Great Danes and bulldogs lived at the kennels side by side with Clumber spaniels, dachshunds, Scotch deer-hounds, black pugs and terriers, Chinese Cows and "Poms" and "Pekes".

Thus a Siberian sledge dog named Luska was once a member of the troupe, a difficult charge, declining to eat meat until enquiry elicited that his normal diet was fish and rice. A Samoyed from an Arctic expedition and a thirteen-stone St. Bernard were other favourites. Then there were tiny Japanese spaniels, huge Basset hounds and an obscure assortment of stray mongrels.

Any dog found wandering without a collar in the Sandringham domain ran the risk of immediate transfer to the kennels until claimed, and many were never claimed. Other dogs were of course personal pets of the royals, Blackie, Zero, Tiny, Muff, Bonny and so many others, destined to end under little headstones at Sandringham or Marlborough House. Brunsdon, the keeper, often had as many as sixty dogs in his charge at a time and the Sandringham kennels, twenty-six in number in a range one hundred yards long, were of an extent matched only by the professional breeder today. But breeding and showing dogs was within the Edwardian scope of royal patronage.

The white doves that fluttered peacefully in Edwardian gardens also owed a degree of popularity to the score kept at Sandringham. The dove house and pigeon-lofts drew interest when a royal pigeon, of Belgian breed, won an international race by homing to Sandringham from the Shetlands, 511 miles in ten hours. "Faster than train," one visitor murmured slyly. It was a cause for secret objection that not all the invited travelled on the Prince's special, which could cover the 98 miles from London to Lynn in just five minutes under two hours.

Guests mainly agreed with Lord Esher that Sandringham was "a deuce of a way from London" but, once arrived, their host steered them briskly from point to point. A morning excursion to the Wolferton stud farm might see much banter in deciding who should drive in the wagonette, who in the Golspie brake, who in a phaeton or in the pale oak pony cart. (As like as not, it came on to rain and the expedition sheltered in the reed-thatched stable before turning back.)

In the afternoon, Sandringham's walks were rarely avoided, except when visitors were nonchalant enough to announce plans of their own or unless, like the Empress Marie of Russia, an individualist made the rounds in a bathchair.

Stout but not torpid, Edward believed in exercise. In his sixties, he still played ice hockey, though inclined to loiter comfortably as goalkeeper. Lawn tennis was one of the few failures at Sandringham and the courts quickly reverted to garden land but placid croquet was perennial, clay-pigeon shooting was introduced by the Duke of York, and the Prince toyed with plans for a golf course.

Perhaps the host, in his anxiety that everyone should find amusement, was apt to harry the lethargic. Even the suggested "little stroll" to the rustic dairy, where a "picnic tea" was occasionally served in a room overlooking the Dutch garden, involved a round of nearly two miles and considerable standing about while the Prince extolled the latest changes in his fruit gardens, greenhouses or farm.

Visiting royalties were flattered and passed the time by planting commemorative trees. The King of Greece found himself at the pigsties of the Home Farm where, rashly admiring the "improved Norfolks", he was instantly presented with a boar and a sow which in due course travelled across Europe together with a Sandringham stockman to tell the Hellenes how the breed should be reared. Liberal politicians were liable to be trudged to West Newton and introduced to the village club, a half-timbered building of some consequence, where each member was permitted to buy a pint of beer a day or "temperance drinks unlimited". It did the radicals no harm to meet working men of the sturdy though respectful Sandringham type or to see the model dwellings that Edward built, the housing of which he boasted personal experience during the only speech he ever made in the House of Lords. The bothy block to house the bachelor gardeners, each with a separate bedroom, was a street in itself, three hundred yards long.

The Sandringham Set, in fact, never precisely matched the fast and loose Marlborough House Set of popular illusion. The Prince's reputation as a Norfolk squire outshone all other auras.

Never as vicious or vulgar, profligate or parvenu as the persistent legends, the Sandringham Set moved in constant flux, often bored for hours on end but always passing the time: the remaining friends of the Prince of Wales' youth, the aristocratic and sporting landlords who entertained him and were entertained in turn, the racing clique, the financiers who could amuse and instruct with City "shop", the newcomers who hesitantly gained friendship in spite of eternal royal clannishness. Sandringham was a social chameleon in the fresh Norfolk air.

Pinning their hopes on the Prince of Wales' known broad morality, a deputation representing 3,258 Norfolk farmers once called at Sandringham to invoke his aid against the law which prohibited marriage with a deceased wife's sister. The Norfolk farmer, though law-abiding and church-going, faced a moral dilemma if his wife died in childbirth, as frequently happened, for the law harshly forbade the widower to wed the one woman in his bereaved household who usually tended his children and took his wife's place in running the home.

The Prince not only saw force in their arguments; he attended Parliament to present the petition, sustained interest both when the Bill was thrown out and when it was revised three years later and continued a prolonged personal and private agitation until in 1896 he used his own vote in the Lords when the Bill reached a third reading. (So much for the modern view that members of the Royal Family must remain aloof from political controversy.) The Bill failed in the Commons but Edward as King finally had the satisfaction of giving the reform his royal assent.

As he increasingly supplemented his mother's duties and created new social fusions of his own, even the success of the

Prince's political parties at Sandringham became an influential and tacitly accepted phenomenon.

The early vogue of the country house weekend as a power centre of politics can be traced as much to Sandringham as its later derivative at Cliveden. Diplomacy, too, drew strength from Sandringham patronage, for there were statesmen and ministers as well as the men of science, artists and musicians, the "very stimulating variety of types" to which John Gore has referred.

The Portuguese minister, the Marquis de Soveral, the "blue monkey" so-called from the invariable hue of his chin, chiefly appears in Sandringham reminiscences for his flirtatious affability with the ladies. But M. Waddington, the French ambassador, was a frequent visitor with his American wife throughout his ten-year term of office; the *entente cordiale* drew nourishment from the first from Sandringham.

M. de Staal, the Russian ambassador, appears and reappears in the house records through nearly a score of years. M. Falbe, the Danish Minister, Count Karolyi as Austrian Ambassador, Baron von Eckardstein of Germany: the list could be lengthened indefinitely. And there were always royal cousins, in-laws, nieces or nephews from every corner of Europe.

The decline of the old century brought once again — in November 1899 — a *rara avis* in the Kaiser, with the Kaiserin, two of their younger sons and an excessive entourage to fill the house to capacity. It was no more than a dismaying chance that the visit coincided with the British reverses that followed the outbreak of the Boer War in South Africa, but the presence of Lord Wolseley, the Commander-in-Chief, among the fellow guests seemed to many a mark of Sandringham secret diplomacy, and a triple alliance of Britain, Germany and the United States was thought to be imminent.

Wilhelm no doubt realised he had absented himself from Sandringham longer even than Queen Victoria. Though still avoiding his Uncle Bertie's birthday, the earlier youthful occasion when he had stormed out of the house and other disagreements remained conveniently buried and outward cordiality was maintained. Wilhelm's appearance on the shooting field was long remembered locally, clad in a hunting suit of pale blue with feathered Tyrolean hat, attended by four jagers, similarly attired, with horns and loaded guns. His one-armed marksmanship however evoked the Duke of York's admiration.

Events now raced towards the twentieth century with increasing momentum. Electric light came to both the "Big House" and York Cottage and in June 1900 the Duke of York could record "Went in Papa's new motorcar. The man managed it extraordinarily well". The Prince of Wales was indeed so convinced of the ultimate triumph of the internal combustion engine that he had already ordered a great sale of carriage horses at Wolferton while prices remained high.

Christmas was celebrated at Sandringham as if it always had been and always would be. In his sixtieth year the Prince could reflect that his Christmas tradition had been established for nearly thirty years and he was approaching his fortieth year as landed proprietor.

The new century in fact found his four York grandchildren quarantined at York Cottage, where the eldest had developed German measles. The Prince of Wales travelled to London on Thursday, January 17th proposing to return to Norfolk for the weekend but it was not to be. The serious news of the Queen's failing strength summoned him to Osborne and when he returned to Sandringham in April 1901 it was as King Edward VII.

III

The King had intended that his first "visit home" should be private. Instead great crowds lined his route from Marlborough House to Liverpool Street Station, at Wolferton a volunteer guard of honour awaited his inspection, and a mounted escort of the Norfolk Yeomanry accompanied the King and Queen to Sandringham House, not without continual difficulty in keeping abreast, two on either side of the carriage, on the narrow road.

At the House nearly all the men of the estate were drawn up, not as tenants and keepers but in uniform as the Sandringham Company of the Norfolk Volunteers. Norfolk pride could not forget that this was the first arrival of the reigning King. But the King and Queen walked down the line, shaking hands, and some "degree of informality"[2] was restored.

Yet the new monarch was already jealous of the dignity of the Crown. His first kingly act at Sandringham was to insist that the bowling alley should be abolished, an act of paternal treachery for, chief skittles exponent of the family, the Duke of York, was abroad on a tour of Australasia and returned to find the alley converted to a library: his unrestrained indignation was one of the few differences ever known between father and son.

Arthur Blomfield, an architect in the royal picture at this time, who had mercilessly restored both Wolferton and West Newton churches, probably had a share in designing this apartment which suggested a bishop's library with its original

---

[2] Royal writers were more fulsome then than now. In describing the Sandringham gardens in the Coronation Number of the Gardeners' Chronicle, a contributor achieved the superb statement, "In the wellhead a rose is planted, and there exists a photograph showing the Queen in the act of affording water to the plant."

coved ceiling and three deep embrasures of books. The beautifully bound presentations to the original north-east library had long since outgrown the shelves. The King had Mr. Humphreys down from Hatchards, the booksellers, to clear out the trash and supply a new range of books "suitable for a country house".

Walking around the park with Frederick Ponsonby, formerly Queen Victoria's assistant private secretary and now his own, the King also ordered the making of the ten-hole golf course that had long been his dream. When he next appeared at Sandringham in the summer, the putting-greens were in established order, the fairways mown, and wicker hurdles had been placed to indicate where the intended bunkers would be dug. The head gardener had placed them at random to left and right of the fairway; the corpulent King drove off, straight into a bunker which he ordered should be placed more to the right and further off the tee.

A strange game followed with the King angrily altering the bunkers at every other tee. A match a day or two later was unnerving. All the hurdles had been moved to the spots the King had indicated; and the monarch angrily asked who had been blundering fool enough to put them there. It was courting disaster to prove from written notes that the King had himself selected the sites. He exploded with wrath and all the hurdles were taken away.

Next season there were only two bunkers on the course but these had been built like gun emplacements. Matches were subsequently played with a Hunstanton professional who was so nervous that the King cursed him freely, convinced that the poor man had been chosen in mistaken loyalty as a bad player who could be readily beaten.

Still more difficult golf was played with Queen Alexandra who confused the game with hockey and, under the impression that one had to prevent an opponent putting the ball in the hole, enjoyed a good scrimmage at every green. In the end the King accepted the hazards resignedly and gave the young Princes, his grandsons, permission to play, though they were strictly forbidden the game at Windsor in case they should hack up the fairway.

Sandringham soon took its accustomed place in the Court itinerary. Ponsonby's early impression had been of a house of mid-Victorian type with polished oak panelling, "masses of photographs on tables but hardly one really good thing in the house". (He had no eye for the Goya tapestries or Indian art.) Closer acquaintance made him aware of the extreme comfort and he extolled the innumerable bathrooms.

Prince Nicholas of Greece also found the drawing-rooms "somewhat old-fashioned in taste and style" but admired the "charming rooms" in the bachelor wing, where "every detail for comfort had been carefully considered". His younger brother, Prince Christopher, at another time enjoyed a room under the clock tower "a bright room with cream-coloured walls and furnished in gay blue and white chintzes".

Yet the young men both marvelled at the clutter of bijouterie accumulating in "Aunt Alix's" rooms, the flagons and scent bottles of every shape and size on her dressing-table, the framed photographs stepping in tiers around her desk, the bogwood Irish charms on the mantelshelf, the white china pigs mixed up with jewelled miracles of Fabergé craftsmanship, the swarming bibelots of every description.

The Queen once asked Christopher to play the piano "properly" for her, which meant raising the lid of the instrument. The lid was covered with masses of photographs which she agreed would take quite an hour to put back, and the Queen was relieved when her nephew discreetly declined.

The astonishing thing is that when the Queen returned to London or to Windsor or went aboard the royal yacht at Cowes, much of her bric-a-brac travelled with her. A stormy sea one night sent her treasures sliding off the table; she sat up half the night replacing them, attempting to stow them safely and mourning the breakages. Her mementos, she insisted, represented the kind thoughts of dear friends: she could not bear to be parted from them.

The speedy and tender packing of baggage constantly undertaken by scores of servants was not the least miracle of Edwardian transport. At Sandringham the guns would crack for a week, the house would gleam with lights and echo with music and conversation, and then, with the cars and wagons piled with luggage, the King and Queen and their guests would clatter away down the drive towards Wolferton and silence descended on the woods and coverts.

At York Cottage the elder children were alone once more with the reality of the tutor, Mr. Hansell, with the blackboard that faced two standard school desks in the schoolroom, with Mama in the evenings and the piano tinkling "Funiculi, Funicula", and the free days of roaming the estate or bicycling to Dersingham, fast and exhilaratingly downhill to buy sweets at Parker's store.

In the new reign three of the York children were still in the nursery stage, but the two eldest boys, Edward and Bertie, the future Duke of Windsor and King George VI, watching their Mama with her embroidery in the evenings, were old enough to learn *gros point*, a hobby that remained a lifelong relaxation for them both.

There were placid afternoons when the boys sat by the lake fishing for roach with bent pins or sometimes navigated the flat-bottomed boat towards the island. Or a gardener, leaning on his spade, would watch the comedy when the boys burst from the house and climbed rapidly into a tree to be followed by their tutor in evident bewilderment at their sudden disappearance. All these, too, were among the facets of Sandringham.

8: THE KING'S HOUSE

I

Sandringham will always glitter in retrospect as the mise-en-scène of the Edwardian era at its brilliant zenith, as if the ladies were always wasp-waisted and witty, bright and beautiful, the gentlemen bluff and urbane, stiff-collared and opportunist. And so they were, at least for part of the time, although the reception rooms were now to know longer periods of solitude and silence, when calico dust-covers replaced the flowers.

As Prince of Wales, Albert Edward once heard the legend of a Danish king condemned to ride through eternity between the two castles where he had been happiest. "In that case," the Prince capped the conversation, "I should be condemned to ride forever between Marlborough House and Sandringham." As King Edward VII, however, he travelled less often between Buckingham Palace and his Norfolk home.

The incessant bustle and pressure of court affairs, the irresistible appeal of the European scene caused the King increasingly to omit his summer weekends at Sandringham and to curtail other visits. His entire reign was to last less than nine years and four months. The tidal flow of royal vitality was ebbing irresistibly towards York Cottage, from which Prince George, the Duke of York, set out on the eve of his father's birthday in Coronation year to welcome the Kaiser once again.

The German emperor had this time consented to honour his uncle's birthday and the King solicitously suggested that his guest should perhaps wear plain clothes "as it is not customary to wear uniforms in the country in England". But his nephew arrived with his accustomed full stiff suite, reinforced by

Counts and Generals as well as gun-bearers and kennelmen, and even cramped York Cottage was called upon to provide extra beds.

Sandringham had never seen hospitality extended more lavishly than for the week's visit; and the house celebrated its fortieth royal year in a jamboree of shooting, entertainment and throne-side diplomacy.

On the King's birthday itself, Kubelik played after dinner, applauded by an audience of two hundred, although Prince George confided to his journal his own involuntary distress at the violinist's long hair.

Next morning the Prince took the Kaiser duck-shooting in the marshes, the sport itself a token of a changing Sandringham, though four days of big partridge and pheasant shoots were held in addition. The Lords Londonderry, Ormonde, Clarendon and Farquhar implemented the guns, while Field Marshal Lord Roberts, the Prime Minister, Mr. Balfour, and the Foreign Minister, Lord Lansdowne, privately conferred at the house.

Politically the statesmen imagined they were tidying up the aftermath of the Boer War rather than sowing the seeds of a further conflict in Europe. The King invited other members of the Cabinet to join the "pourparlers", as they were called, but these new recruits happened to include the Kaiser's pet detestation, Joseph Chamberlain, and a faint edge marred the atmosphere.

Albert Chevalier was among the entertainers one night and the Germans may have stirred restively at his Cockney dirge, "My Old Dutch" or scented offence in being offered so "low" a comedian. Unspoken perils of mischance and disaster fringed every circumstance. The Kaiser looked suspiciously at some dietetic pills recommended by his hostess. "Does the silly man think I shall poison him?" said the Queen. Horace Goldin, the illusionist, travelled down with his mass of magical impediments for the Queen's amusement, an entertainment ideally chosen, for Queen Alexandra exclaimed loudly at every live fish produced wriggling from the air and remembered the card tricks with precision.

At a repeat performance years later, she reminded Goldin, "Last time it was the nine of clubs, now it's the five of hearts." On the other hand, Goldin created tension during his performance by requesting the Kaiser to tie two handkerchiefs together. Fortunately, the conjuror realised the difficulty of the withered arm in time and adroitly murmured, "But perhaps you had better watch the Queen, sir," and those nearby relaxed with a sense of danger averted.

On the final evening the King attempted to excel himself by "commanding" Sir Henry Irving to give a performance of Conan Doyle's play *Waterloo*. Irving's company were playing that week in Belfast and their journey entailed a special ship for the sea crossing, an express railway connection and two special trains.

Even so a detail was almost fatally overlooked in the complex plans. The play depended on the dramatic beat of the kettledrum for the culminating moment when the dying veteran struggles from his chair. Reliance was placed on the royal orchestra and it turned out that the Sandringham string band did not include a drummer.

Consternation prevailed until the police sergeant remembered that one of his men played the kettledrum in the police band, but the constable was absent on a distant beat. Horses were sent and the musical policeman retrieved; but a worse crisis occurred when the temperamental Sandringham conductor saw the score at the very last moment and decided he could not play it.

At this very instant the royalties were entering the room. The stage manager seized a violin bow and brought it down with at least the necessary gesture of showmanship for the overture and the performance, of course, passed without a hitch.

But it had been a near thing, and the actors were not to know that the underlying tension matched the mood of the house-party. The Queen wrote after the Kaiser's final departure that she was "perfectly exhausted" and the King was heard to groan, "Thank God he's gone."

The ensuing Court Circular resembled a playbill, for the King generously allowed the complete programme to be reprinted, with the names of the cast and list of scenes. This practice being also followed for subsequent productions, a command performance was all the more regarded as a great honour and the Sandringham theatricals were a distinguishing feature of the reign.

On Alexandra's own first birthday as Queen, in accession year, the King designed an appropriate surprise by engaging Sousa and his band. Though mercifully not at its full strength of eighty-four men, the band threatened to blow the audience from their seats. But the deaf Queen sat entranced, beating time, for she could hear every note: the *Stars and Stripes*, *Washington Post*, *El Capitan*, a programme of at least seven marches and seven encores. The choice typified the King's thoughtfulness as a husband, but the Queen's disability remained a secret, to the dismay of comedians who chanced to catch sight of her unamused expression.

The first Sandringham stage performance of the reign came a fortnight after Sousa's visit when the Queen laughed obligingly at Dan Leno. No doubt she was told afterwards of his wisecrack on being shown round the garden, "Why, this is a bigger place than mine!" Leno shared a double bill with Seymour Hicks and Ellaline Terriss, who appeared in *Scrooge* and *Papa's Wife* and at supper the delightful Ellaline happened to admire the set of exquisite hen-shaped salt and pepper cellars, only to be immediately presented with them by the impetuous Queen, as well as an intended presentation brooch set in diamonds, rubies and emeralds.

More than thirty years later Miss Terriss could exactly recall the wonderment of a visit to the kitchens, "I have never seen their equal. In one corner ducks, woodcocks, snipe and other wildfowl were being roasted on an enormous spit, whilst a contingent of chefs basted them. We seemed to have stepped right back into the middle ages."

Others remembered the difficulties of the improvised ballroom stage where scene changes took time, for scene-cloths and battens had to be hung without marking the walls. In the naval production *The Flag Lieutenant* C. Aubrey Smith was supposed to collapse wounded on the deck and feared that he might misjudge his fall and hurtle into the King's lap. The only accident, however, was in a battleship scene when he bumped his head against one of the supposed twelve-inch guns, which thereupon shivered visibly in its bearings, reducing the audience to helpless laughter.

Other scaled-down Sandringham productions included Charles Hawtrey in *The Man From Blankley's* and the same effective actor in *The Little Damozel* by Monckton Hoffe, but if special scenery had to be painted, no one was concerned with expense. An account sheet has survived showing that it cost £233 14s. 6d. to present Sir George Alexander in a Christmas production of Sutro's *The Builder of Bridges* in 1908. This compares favourably with a bill at about the same time for

£206 — including £26 "hire of film and projector" — for a motion picture entertainment.

The movies had however flickered at Sandringham as early as 1900 as an overture to the twentieth century. "After dinner last night we had the Biograph or moving photographs in the ballroom" wrote the future King George V. "Some of them were marvellously good... We had the Biograph again and it was even better than the first night. All the people round and servants came to see it."

Yet this was not the only harbinger of the modern age. At Sandringham in 1906 the King put on a pair of headphones and listened to a crackling, squeaky cacophony alleged to be Melba singing in the last act of an opera at Covent Garden.

The King's Lynn-London trunk telephone circuit had been linked to "the Electrophone Exchange", we are told, to achieve a minor miracle. "The articulation of the artistes however was poor", and the King asked if he could hear something of the musical comedies *See See* and *The Dairymaids* at the Prince of Wales and Apollo theatres.

The following morning, being Sunday, it was the turn of the Queen and her spinster daughter, Princess Victoria, to attempt to hear the closing hymns from St. Michael's, Chester Square, Cole Abbey and other churches. Unluckily, the sermon from St. Michael's did not come over as well as it should have done because the choirboys were secretly stuffing the sleeves of their surplices into the microphones to see what would happen. The Electrophone Company did not change the world, despite their ingenuity in involving the King and Queen in their publicity.

II

Fixed on the stage of its own dimension of time, the Sandringham scene of this richest Edwardian phase varies with the viewpoint of each member of its audience. The sharp eyes of Margot, the Countess of Oxford and Asquith, did not admire the yellow polished oak of the entrance hall of Sandringham House with "inferior portraits of the Royal Family … inserted in the panels".

She considered it noteworthy that every chair and sofa was upholstered with red and blue striped linen "to represent the Guards' colours", though others remarked that the scheme was the red, blue and gold of the King's racing colours. Margot Oxford noticed also that no one appeared quite at their ease with royalty.

The Prince of Wales, affable yet commanding, had been one personality, but the King was another, sharper and graver of mien. Intervals of sudden silence fell between spurts of lively general conversation. Gottlieb's string orchestra could take up the slack, thrumming their Viennese waltzes in the balcony, playing, "like a bee in a bottle", as Frederick Ponsonby said, for an hour.

But arriving travellers could now use the ballroom entrance without bursting informally upon the tea party: they would otherwise have found the women in tea-gowns, the men in short black jackets, striped trousers and black ties, rather like a convention of glossy company directors, but all munching egg sandwiches or brioches or chocolate cake.

Gottlieb's discreet vanishing was always the signal for the initiated to tiptoe to the library, to read or talk, while others might still loiter about the hall with backgammon and other games.

The King withdrew upstairs to his own room, a more masculine version of the Queen's own cluttered apartments, littered with photographs and big game trophies, still furnished with the mahogany pieces brought back from the *Serapis* after his cruise to India some thirty years before. But His Majesty was still apt to tour the guest wings, stepping into a guest-room ostensibly to poke the fire and surreptitiously perhaps to satisfy his curiosity.

The room was not always found unoccupied. Hearing him at the door, Admiral Fisher mistook him for a footman and roared "Come in! Don't go humbugging with the door handle," and the King discovered his first Sea Lord with a boot in each hand. But the conversation was to be duly noted down for posterity.

"What on earth are you doing?"

"Unpacking, sir."

"Where's your servant?"

"Haven't got one, sir!"

"Where is he?"

"Never had one! Couldn't afford it!"

Then the King sat down companionably until, with only fifteen minutes to go before dinner time, the Admiral reminded him, "Sir, you'll be angry if I'm late for dinner. No doubt your Majesty has two or three gentlemen to dress you, but I have no one." The King, as Fisher ever afterwards remembered, gave "a sweet smile" at thus being turned out of a room in his own house.

Dinner was at half-past eight Greenwich time or at nine by the Sandringham clocks. The Gottlieb musicians were within earshot; the ladies wore tiaras, the gentlemen sparkled with ribands and decorations; the harsh Goya tapestries of the dining-room receded muted in the general brilliance. There were six candelabra, each with four candles. The electric light glowed upon the mass of silver on the sideboard, on the polished array of Mogul armour and weapons displayed above the mantelshelf: everywhere light glittered and the table was often set for as many as twenty-eight covers.

The King practised the habit of taking a different lady into dinner each evening. The conversation, one gathers, had a general flow and gaiety not found at teatime, though few remembered the bon mots, after the glow of the wine. *Queen Alexandra*: "I do so like soldiers. I ought to have been a nursemaid." Or someone mentions that Cleopatra is not among his favourite characters in history, a phrase repeated loudly to the Queen, who responds, "And I should hope *not*!" Or another lady is sometimes at the table, Mrs. George Keppel, the King's mistress, Junoesque, "kind-hearted to a high degree, clever in witty repartee", we are told by the reticent Sidney Lee, the King's biographer.

They are ghosts now and we can only stand like ghosts ourselves, deaf and dumb, craning around the dinner-table, glimpsing Mrs. Willie James or Lady Troubridge or Mrs. Cornwallis-West, the Arthur Sassoons, the Duke and Duchess of Devonshire, Sir Ernest Cassel or others less enhanced by notoriety, like Felix Semon, the King's physician, and so many more.

And of course Portugal's ubiquitous Soveral, so welcome to Sandringham that when his name was accidentally omitted from the list the King telegraphed him and demanded on his arrival, "Why did you wait for an invitation?" One does not intrude unasked but the popular diplomat blandly capped the moment by remarking, "Well, sir, I had got as far as my door when your command arrived!"

Dinner rarely lasted more than an hour, twelve to fourteen courses of the elaborate menu depended on faultless service, replacing the remnants of *Cutlets á la Dubarry* with *Poulet Danoise* and presently *Caisses de fraises Miramare*.

After the dessert and coffee, bridge became the fashion, the King walking round the tables to ensure that everyone was engaged. (The drawing-room was so cluttered with bijouterie that tables were generally set out in the ballroom or library.) Yet no lady could retire until the Queen rose to leave. Her departure was then a signal for a feminine procession towards the landings, little groups dissolving and reforming, stopping to laugh and chatter. The gentleman too could not retire until the King.

There were light snacks at midnight, and bridge or talk resuming, usually, till after one in the morning. There is a sad little tale of how the seventy-five-year-old General Sir Dighton Probyn was once found to be absent. He had felt unwell but had failed to make his excuses and the poor man was aroused from sleep and told the King wanted him.

And so to the distant cockcrow and clattering of blinds that announced another day, the meeting with the children on the garden paths, the pleasant loitering, the amusement of photography unless, as so often, the incredible slaughter of a shoot was in progress.

John Burns, the first Labour leader to gain Cabinet rank, was a visitor one weekend, and the King proudly displayed to him the apple store near the farm, with its endless array of shelving, while a contingent of royal children followed them round.

Apple after apple was passed to Burns to inspect and handed surreptitiously by him to the royal princes — the future George VI, the Duke of Windsor and the Duke of Gloucester no doubt among them. The King, having sternly ordered them not to touch the apples, was startled to find their hands full of forbidden fruit. "Who gave them to you?" he demanded.

"I did," said Burns. "As President of the Local Government Board, I am the authority for outdoor relief." No doubt the

King guffawed. His eyes also probably twinkled with mischief when he walked none other than Archbishop Lang through the snow one Sunday to inspect Persimmon at the racing stud. But the Archbishop was impressed.

"His Magnificence dwells in a separate house padded with yellow leather and carefully regulated in temperature, with his own establishment of tutors and governors," he recounted in a letter home. "We then went through the magnificent conservatories built of Persimmon's Derby winnings, under the guidance of the inevitable intelligent Scottish gardener."

The gardens, too, had now nearly assumed their maximum opulence. The King once told Admiral Fisher that if he could have followed a private professional life, he would have chosen the career of landscape gardener. Early in the reign crowds would often collect at the Norwich Gates to stare down the drive towards the house, though fortunately the vista was blocked by the ancient and splendid lime trees, the self-same trees once known to Mr. Motteux, which now towered nearly as high as the mansion itself.

In 1907, however, a terrible gale blew down many of the trees and so ravaged the rest that all were condemned as unsafe. When they were felled, sightseers gained a direct view of the windows of the King's private rooms. This suggested to their monarch that privacy could be restored if a high wall replaced the Norwich Gates and if these were moved to a new easterly position to form an entrance facing the front door.

The scheme was drawn up and announced with a flourish, only to be awkwardly countermanded a few weeks later. The King had failed to consult the Queen on his summary disposal of their joint wedding gift, and Queen Alexandra was evidently so angry and voiced her objections so indignantly that the King's proposals were cancelled. Instead, her husband had no option but to work out an agreeable alternative, which was far more costly.

The great Norwich Gates were moved bodily three hundred yards farther north from the house and the road leading from Wolferton to Anmer was then diverted, the park walls taken down and rebuilt and trees planted until the house was again concealed from view. This was King Edward VII's last great alteration.

III

The highwater mark of the Sandringham visits was — as it is still — the Sandringham Christmas... Dickens in a Cartier setting, as the Duke of Windsor neatly said.

The festivities began on the afternoon of Christmas Eve when the King, knickerbockered and cloaked, arrived with his family at the stable yard, where all the tenant-workers of the estate were waiting, some three hundred people, gamekeepers, foresters, gardeners, herdsmen, stablehands, or their wives, ready to file into the coach-house.

The King took his seat inside, near the door, and beyond was a gory sight the royal children long remembered: a vista of scores of large and bloody joints of beef on trays, marshalled on long tables which were covered by white cloths, each joint tagged with the name of the intended recipient, one for each family.

As the workers walked out with their meat, the King wished each a happy Christmas, and the men touched their caps, the women bobbed, until the babble of conversation, always hushed in the coach-house, was released again in the open air. These were only the outdoor servants; the turn of the indoor staff, in those days, came on New Year's Eve.

After the meat distribution, the royal children hurried home to tea and to change their clothes for party-going. Up at the Big House they presently joined the family in the salon, where the crash of a gong heralded the obliging arrival of Santa Claus from the mysterious nether regions of the steward's room, first to bow to the King and Queen and then to lead the royal family in procession to the ballroom.

In that vast apartment, the Christmas tree nearly scraped the lofty ceiling. Ranged round the walls were linen-covered tables heaped with presents, with space allotted for each person, in some order and degree of precedence.

Thus the table for the King and Queen stood nearest to the Christmas tree, the children's tables in a remote corner. This arrangement was essentially practical for it avoided the risk of some precious novelty — sent from the Czar by special messenger, or one of the jewelled Fabergé animals, which the King often gave to the Queen — becoming the casualty of some childish popgun.

With agonising suspense, the children received their presents last. First came the higher officials of the Household, led by old Sir Dighton Probyn, looking increasingly like Santa Claus himself, then the secretaries and equerries, some finding the lavish generosity an ordeal. "One found the King on one side and the Queen on the other explaining who gave what present and giving particulars about the various articles," says Sir Frederick Ponsonby. "One stood gasping one's thanks to each alternately."

Before the flow of gifts were reduced to sweets and bonbons and the children honked their toy motors through a sea of wrapping paper, hundreds of presents were exchanged. Hardly was this lavish celebration over than the carol singers arrived from the village to sing in the salon and for several evenings afterwards it became the house-party habit to go to the ballroom, an emporium of dazzling gifts, to inspect one another's presents.

The festive season was diversified, too, by the plays and concerts and vaudeville performances. The Zancigs came one snowy year to demonstrate their thought-transference act and of course performed their tricks as readily in Danish for their fellow-Dane, the Queen, as in English. A heavy snowfall trapped them at the house overnight but they used the telephone with such good effect on the newspapers that their publicity incurred a royal letter of rebuke, "His Majesty thought that far too many details of your demonstrations appeared in the newspapers..."

New Year's Eve brought another present-giving when the ballroom tables were rearranged and the indoor servants filed in to receive their own royal supply of gift packages. There is a charming story of how Queen Alexandra once found a footman gazing moodily out of the window. "You look lonely," she said. "No one must be lonely in my house at Christmas," and thereupon presented him with a pair of golf cufflinks. "These are a personal gift from me to you," she explained. "You will get your ordinary presents at the Tree."

The servants handed over numbered tickets while the King or the Princess eagerly hunted the corresponding surprise from the tree. Tschumi, the chef, has told how he received half a dozen silver forks one year, six silver knives the next, until a canteen of cutlery was complete, but not every gift always reached the ideal recipient. A housemaid might open her package to discover a razor. A valet was given perfume. Mistakes were ironed out later.

The Queen also instituted a fancy-dress staff ball, an idea economically adopted by a group of footmen who dressed up as members of a shooting party. "A capital entertainment!" the Queen told Lady Battersea. "It means three weeks of amusing preparation and as long after the event in talking it over, and then in being photographed in costume."

Not that the Queen's ideas were shared throughout the hierarchy of Edwardian servants. "I never dress up," the housekeeper once said indignantly. "I leave that to the under-servants."

IV

There were no legends of ghosts to enhance the Sandringham Christmas spirit. The only spook ever sighted was allegedly seen in high summer by Prince Christopher of Greece. This occurred in one of the modern bedrooms near the clock tower where, while resting on his bed before dressing for dinner, the Prince saw, so he claimed, the head of a young and beautiful woman framed in his dressing-table mirror, a woman wearing a little black mask, through which her eyes gazed "with a depth of sad entreaty".

It must have been difficult to see so much, but it made a good story. The Prince rushed downstairs to tell his sister, Princess Marie, and Princess Victoria; he had felt rooted to the bed with fear, his valet had passed within inches of the figure without seeing her. While Marie giggled, Princess Victoria said firmly that he was overtired and ought to take a tonic. But even princes sometimes need to impress people. Visiting Houghton the next day the Prince professed to recognise the lady of the mirror in the portrait of an ancestress of one of the Cholmondeleys. She wore the identical dress in which she had appeared to Christopher, she was holding the self-same little mask.

It would have been remarkable, of course, if Christopher had seen a Flemish face in a starched cap so near to the forgotten room above the old kitchen that had long held the eerie portrait of the Flemish martyr. But knowing nothing of the Hostes, Christopher elected for the Cholmondeley lady who was "never spoken of" and had "died of a broken heart" and we need not take him too seriously.

Perhaps the true ghosts were, after all, the ghosts of time, the fleeting years, so nearly as transitory as the white dust that rose and fell on the Wolferton road in the wake of the chugging motorcars.

The Queen was a little more frequently at Sandringham on her own, that is with old Sir Dighton Probyn and her own faithful Charlotte Knollys, as if forming a tighter protective enclave against the closing dusk. The King always concluded his Christmas visit promptly with the New Year, and was off and away, to enjoy hospitality and shooting elsewhere.

The winter sojourn and his incessant cigars did not improve the King's bronchial catarrh. In moods of deep melancholy he sometimes talked of abdication. The gloom of his sixty-eighth birthday, his last at Sandringham, was particularly marked, for the King's old friend, Montagu Guest, suddenly fell dead in the shooting field.

The King, shocked, lost his customary presence of mind. Rugs were laid over the body on the muddy ground but the King sent his chauffeur, Stamper, to "look and make sure". He thought of trying to get a motor vehicle into the morass of field before he recollected himself and the horse-drawn ambulance was summoned. That night Lord Rosebery found it a difficult task to propose the health of the King.

Later in November, the Royal Family were again at Sandringham, still not fully shaking off the sense of ill omen.

The King went to Appleton House, to see his son-in-law, King Haakon of Norway and Queen Maud; he was driven to East Dereham to buy Christmas presents from an antique dealer. He moved about the countryside as if taking stock of each scene, and Christmas, and then the New Year of 1910, found him at the house as usual.

He last visited Sandringham on April 30th, but Queen Alexandra was then in Corfu and the housekeeper received instructions not to open up the drawing-rooms for the weekend. It was a bachelor party with Probyn, Ponsonby and four or five others, and the King was no sooner out of the warm train than he loitered about in the cold wind in the garden, looking at some alterations with Beck, the agent, and Cook, the head-gardener.

The next day he felt sufficiently out-of-sorts not to join the others in walking the short distance to church but drove there in a carriage. Then after lunch he walked once again round his beloved estate, inspecting the planting, though the weather was still bitterly cold and rainy.

Afterwards the King sat, going through some routine work, in his secretary's workroom, that bleak little room near the stairs, though there was no fire in the grate in the corner and it struck others as chilly. Sandringham had never been more malignant. Next morning, May 2nd, he left for London coughing with the onset of bronchitis. Four days later, King Edward VII died, without attaining the looming landmark of a half-century of Sandringham ownership.

9: THE DOWER HOUSE

I

In the summer of 1910 Queen Alexandra the Queen Mother retired to Sandringham for a few months, and her son, the new King George V, wrote to her tenderly from Balmoral, "You must miss beloved Papa terribly at dear Sandringham which he created and where you have spent so many happy years of your life".

At the end of October, the dowager Queen was with her sister in Denmark and the King came down to Sandringham for a few days shooting but the only change he effected in estate affairs was to take over Park House, west of the church, for his staff and guests. King Edward VII had left Sandringham House to Queen Alexandra for her lifetime and the new King would not have dreamed of contravening his father's will, although the consequent difficulties of his own staff arrangements were to cost him several thousands a year.

His Prime Minister, Mr. Asquith, visited Sandringham in November to find the King still working at York Cottage, in his "red-flannelled" study just inside the front door. The absurd little house, the one-time Bachelors' Cottage, as cramped and inconvenient as ever, was now occupied by the King and Queen and their family of six, and as many of their staff as could be squeezed in, but the new reign brought about no other change.

As assistant secretary, Sir Frederick Ponsonby was asked by Queen Mary if he could use the schoolroom as his office. He agreed but the schoolroom, it turned out, was the one place where the younger generation — Prince Edward (the Duke of

178

Windsor) Prince Albert (later George VI) Prince Henry (the Duke of Gloucester) and the others — were accustomed to meet and talk. The secretary gathered up his papers and resorted to the billiard room. Here also he was disturbed by two teenage princes eager for a game, and he retreated to his bedroom.

Calling to discuss police arrangements, the Chief Constable of Norfolk was surprised to find the King's secretary coping with papers between a brass bedstead and a small writing table. Other business visitors, awaiting their turn on the landing, were startled to overhear every word on the telephone in the hall downstairs, one of the only two in the house.

The King's old friend, Charles Cust, privately commented that it was quite absurd for the Big House to be inhabited by an old lady and her daughter while everyone squeezed into tiny York Cottage. Princess Victoria thought the criticism very unkind, and carried the tale, and the King asked Cust bluntly what the devil it had to do with him.

Even Queen Mary ventured to point out that it was impractical for the King and Queen not to have room for a single guest. But to all this the King replied urbanely, "It is my mother's home. My father built it for her" and so silenced all criticism.

At the same time he often said he did not know where his servants lived: he supposed "in the trees". They were mainly billeted at West Newton. They crowded into Park House. They occupied the old Folly, the breezy balconied cottage a mile nearer the station. They rarely intruded, except by special arrangement, into the bachelor rooms of the Big House.

The Christmas of Accession Year was spent at Sandringham, the younger family driving up from the Cottage and the King gravely noted, "Mother dear gave us all our presents in the ballroom as usual. We missed beloved papa too dreadfully."

King George had however supervised the meat distribution at the coach-house, meeting his tenantry, and in the New Year, Frank Beck presented a satisfactory account of estate affairs. There seemed, indeed, no need of major changes. The herds of pedigree shorthorns and Red Polls, with Irish Dexters and Jerseys and with the Southdown sheep, provided a satisfactory farming policy.

The breeding of Sandringham shire horses remained an asset. At the racehorse stud, dominated by the enormous bronze statue of Persimmon, a trio of retired stallions handsomely paid expenses and, on the racing side, the new King was to enjoy a promising winner in the month before his Coronation.

In the game coverts, too, it is estimated that Bland, the keeper, reared over a million head of game in the years before the 1914–18 war, and the new King felt no inclination to change his father's prodigious tradition. Joining forces with Lord Farquhar at Castle Rising, the King and his friends enjoyed access to thirty thousand acres of shooting. The King was rightly ranked one of the best shots in England. Yet his own preferences already presaged the new, more informal trends.

He enjoyed a long tramp into the marshes with perhaps only an equerry as companion, picking up what might come, and perhaps a following day in the bracken clearings, where the woodcock were most likely to be flushed. High and erratic in flight, the elusive woodcock was to be judged a fit opponent, and the quality of the pheasant shooting was gradually, almost imperceptibly, sacrificed to this keener sport.

For company, too, the King was as happy with neighbours and farmers whose names — Mr. Stanton, Mr. Bullard, Mr.

Brereton — henceforth frequently appear in the game books. "The keenest man on a woodcock I ever knew," Mr. Brereton once said of the King. "Our rivalry was a good joke between us. If I missed a woodcock, the King wouldn't fail to tell me of it. If he missed one … well, he wouldn't tell me…"

King George V's sons, especially David (the Duke of Windsor) and Bertie (George VI) also brought fresh elements to the sporting scene. "My first day with a party," the future George VI began an account of a January day in 1910 when, shooting with his father, George Brereton and three others, a bag of 312 pheasants, thirty-six hares, three rabbits, etc. was recorded. But when out shooting with his brother, through the fir plantations at Christmas 1911 he was able to record the extra triumph, "December 27th. My first woodcock."

II

While the new King and Queen were absent in India for their Durbar visit during the winter of 1911–1912, the residents at York Cottage were reduced to Prince Edward and the three younger children. Remembering their parents' instruction to look after their grandmother, however, they often walked up the slight rise, past the lake, to call on Queen Alexandra. They would sit shouting to her amid all her confused relics or help her to play patience or fit another segment into her jigsaw puzzle.

She was now within sight of her seventieth year, the "Sea King's Daughter" who had come to England so long ago, and to her youthful callers her household seemed much older than it was. White-bearded and bent, General Sir Dighton Probyn crept about, Miss Knollys sat hunched in her ever-watchful corner, and it was Queen Alexandra's unmarried daughter,

Princess Victoria — Aunt Toria to the younger generation — who seemed in real and effective charge of the mansion.

The trophies of Omdurman, brought back by Kitchener from the Sudan, ranged up the staircase, fascinating to the children when luridly glowing red with reflections from the stained glass windows. An odd array of Matabeleland trophies commanded an upper passage and it was always Aunt Toria who sharply found fault. An army of domestics grappled with the rust that constantly threatened the Indian armour or strove to keep some order in the stacks of fraying photographs, seeking some space to flick a feather duster among the dense mass of bibelots.

As if aware that there was at last too much clutter, Queen Alexandra was apt to press gifts on all and sundry. Christmas and birthdays would see Copenhagen china discreetly weeded out. Children were given toys from an unfailing store. A glimpse of a child or a venturesome gypsy crossing the lawns was sufficient to send her hobbling out with a gift.

The Queen was suspected of keeping her spies at the kitchen door where tramps would sometimes triumphantly appear, after breaking through the lodge defences at West Newton. If a whisper of their presence reached Alexandra, she sent out alms, despite protestations. She felt indeed that her staff was wrong in trying to prevent her and she enjoyed pitting her generosity against the guile of her protectors.

The sight of a postman often meant a race between the Queen and her lady-in-waiting to seize any begging letters. "Poor man," the Queen would say, "send him ten pounds." Miss Knollys might plead, "But, Ma'am, he has just come out of prison for theft!" Persuasions were idle. "Poor man, he'll need money all the more. Send him twenty pounds."

The Dowager Empress Marie of Russia came to stay and the two widowed elderly sisters, still dressed very alike, so long familiar in the Sandringham scene, had an air of novelty as if both had assumed new character roles.

As they hobbled about, shouting to one another in Danish, an incongruous touch was added by the Empress's personal guard, an immensely tall, bearded Cossack in full costume, who followed her everywhere with impassive devotion. The Empress, alas, found that the Sandringham rain unfailingly implied lumbago. "Thank God you have got over your lumbago," the Czar Nicholas wrote to his mother, as the dampness dried in high summer. "What a nuisance it always happens to you in England."

The walk of Empress and Queen to the kennels, covered by huge white aprons, carrying baskets of bread for the excited dogs, also had a grotesque formality that convulsed younger nephews and nieces. The Queen would pause before a rose and bend her head over it gracefully. The Empress would then do the same with added pathos. The Queen would then sweep her hand in a gesture of summons, as if to say, "Come and smell!" and her guests and escorts would inhale obediently.

When the two ageing ladies went riding, almost anyone they found walking on the roads would be swept into their landau. A boy confessed that his father was a local poacher. "Poor man," said the Queen, "then I shall send him a hamper."

In summer the Ponsonby children were apt to be transported from Park House to the Queen's bungalow on the seashore at Snettisham, and the former Loelia Ponsonby has given us a candid child's eye picture. "The Queen was so deaf that conversation was impossible and we thought her nice but boring... Queen Alexandra wore a toque and a veil speckled with black spots through which one could see a dazzling auburn wig... She had a bunch of artificial parma violets pinned to her somewhere, and while we splashed about in the water she stood on the beach, a strange, improbable and yet graceful figure, which all too soon waved a parasol as a sign we were to come out." The mention of the wig would not have upset the Queen. Finding it askew, she was always ready to pat it back into place and cry gaily, "Is it straight, dear child?"

But these eccentricities deepened at times into vague dottiness. Unprepared visitors were embarrassed when, as frequently happened, she emotionally dragged the long-dead Duke of Clarence into the conversation, as if he had been gone only months instead of a score of years. "Eddy was not handsome; he was far from robust," she would buttonhole a friend. "'Man looketh on the countenance, but God on the heart' is what I had engraved on his tomb."

The long sorrowing mother could not be persuaded at times not to regard her second son as a usurper and it was noticed that she inscribed envelopes to him as "King George" instead of, correctly, "The King". Prince Eddy's room near the clock tower was still set apart, never used, with its floral offerings.

But now there was a second locked chamber, to which friends could be taken on hushed and mournful visits. In the late King's apartments, as in Eddy's room, nothing had been changed. In his bedroom, the bed was made up, his clothing hanging as if to be worn. With close friends, raising a finger to her lips the old Queen would point silently to an enlarged photograph of Mrs. Keppel which she had hung significantly over the door.

Meanwhile, King Edward's white terrier Caesar padded about the house. On his collar was inscribed "I am Caesar; I belong to the King". Members of the Household sometimes pointed him out to visitors as "le célèbre" but Queen

Alexandra occasionally regarded him with revulsion. "Horrid little dog!" she told Margot Oxford. "He never went near my poor husband when he was ill." Caesar died in April 1914.

III

The New Year of 1914 began well at the Big House. "We all dined with Mama" Queen Mary recorded, and the young people danced afterwards, again breaking the mournful silence of years. In the frosty weather the King went shooting at Anmer: "more pheasants than I have ever seen there, we got 2,831."

On August 4th, when war was declared, the Royal Family was in London amid the tumult of the excited crowds. At Sandringham the wind beat steadily against the house all day but with the evening a stillness fell except for the chuckling of the blackbirds among the shrubs and the flighting of duck towards the ponds.

It was late autumn before the King and Queen could return to this peace and snatch five days at York Cottage. For the next five years their only break from the business of State and duty was to be the short Christmas holiday in Norfolk; the only shooting was for the benefit of the hospitals and farmers; the few remaining carriage horses were sent for ambulance work and Queen Alexandra, who always enjoyed a showy horse, was served by a hack almost too old for his task.

After Christmas, when rumours of an intended enemy invasion were rife, a guard of 120 Grenadiers joined the King and Queen. What happened however was an unexpected Zeppelin foray. While the maids were sitting listening to the gramophone after tea, someone heard the whizzing drone of the aircraft crossing the park.

Everyone rushed outside into the darkness and a curious dull thudding was heard a long way off. One of the bombs dropped by the raider carved a hole towards the Wolferton flats. In later years, when it filled up with water, duck began to frequent it casually. King George VI realised its sporting possibilities and in 1937 the waterhole was extended to form the pool known as Wolferton Splash.

This uncertain cruise of the Zeppelin L.4. was in fact the first German air raid of the war. Its hoped-for effect might be gauged from the headlines of the pro-German *Milwaukee Free Press*, "Zeppelins Bombard Sandringham as King George and The Queen flee. Panic Grips Capital."

Scattering bombs from Hunstanton southward, the raider in reality did little harm except at King's Lynn, where four were killed, and seventeen, including three children, injured. Next day, villagers chattered of "the biggest sausage" they had ever seen but, after this, two naval guns were sited at Sandringham.

As it turned out, no further local hostilities occurred yet when the King next "came home" at the turn of 1915–1916, it was himself as a war invalid, after the accident in France when his horse took fright at the cheering troops and reared on top of him, fracturing his pelvis.

At Christmas the family tried to cheer him up with comic songs; and played ragtime on the gramophone. But there were also wounded for the Queen to visit at the cottage hospital, and an atmosphere of tense anxiety and bereavement was spreading through the estate. Many of the men of the Sandringham contingent were reported missing after the Gallipoli disasters, Frank Beck among them, and were never seen again.

Prince Albert (George VI) was invalided home with the gastric illness that plagued his wartime career, fretting at not "doing his bit", and he recovered to take part in the Battle of Jutland. During one of these sick-leaves, he shot a stag in the park that had become dangerous, and presumably stewed venison was a welcome addition to the menu.

The flower gardens vanished under rows of vegetables cultivated by land girls, but much of the produce was diverted elsewhere. The King and Queen rationed themselves and their household drastically. Anyone late for breakfast at York Cottage got nothing — and one was late if the clock sounded while one was on the stairs. Hungry secretaries found it advisable to enter the dining-room a little beforehand.

An equerry who was detained on the telephone one morning dared to ring the bell in the dining-room and ask for a boiled egg. "If he had ordered a dozen turkeys he could not have made a bigger stir," Sir Frederick Ponsonby relates. "The King accused him of unpatriotic behaviour and went so far as to hint that we should lose the war on account of his gluttony."

But this was in lighter mood. Every letter to York Cottage soon seemed to bring news of a close friend or the son of a friend who had been killed. As the tide of blood flowed on, the Queens and their ladies used to spend long afternoons picking up horse chestnuts which served some mystic purpose at munition factories and they supervised the collection of scrap iron, jam jars and old glass bottles in every neighbouring village. It was all that could be done around Sandringham itself.

The final German offensive on the Western Front matched the news that cousin Nicky (the Czar) and all his family had been shot by the Bolsheviks. It seemed a miracle that Queen Alexandra's sister, the Empress Marie Feodorovna, was allowed to stay under guard at her villa beside the Black Sea. The black news that was expected never came, and the

Empress, still with her faithful guardian Cossack, was rescued by Allied warships in 1919 and brought safely to Sandringham.

The heartfelt relief of the coming of peace was, however, darkened for Queen Mary and the King by the death at Wood Farm, Wolferton, of their youngest son, the epileptic boy, Prince John. The doctors had judged it best that he should live alone with his devoted nurse, Mrs. Bill; the intensity of his attacks had been increasing and the Queen could only write with resignation of "a great release". The King perforce spent the Christmas of 1918 in London.

It was not until the Christmas of 1919 that the whole family was reunited once more at York Cottage, going up to their old grandmother at the Big House just as usual.

The twenty-five-year-old Prince of Wales (the Duke of Windsor) was fresh with the laurels of his successful tour in Canada, and Albert was made Duke of York a few months later. Neither Prince Albert nor Prince Henry had far to come home from Cambridge.

The family had grown up, the third generation at Sandringham. The Big House had grown shabbier and quieter. Damp seeped into the ballroom, and woodworm and decay crept unnoticed into the more distant bedrooms.

There is a story of a young guest in the house who always went to bed at an early hour, whenever Charlotte Knollys shuffled in, bent and now in her late eighties, to pass the rest of the evening with Queen Alexandra. The young guest, one evening, was disturbed by the silence that reigned in the house and, with the inkling of dread that sometimes possesses those alone with the old, she got out of bed and went as she was, in curlpapers and dressing-gown to investigate. She stole down the stairs and along the corridors but heard no sound. She waited outside the Queen's boudoir and still all was silent. She turned the door handle and softly went in. The Queen and old Charlotte were sitting on either side of the fire, both fast asleep.

But if the Big House was hushed, the piano thrummed cheerfully at York Cottage and the gramophone blared its foxtrots and tangos across the lawn. In November 1921, thirty-nine-year-old Lord Lascelles was staying in the house and proposed to Princess Mary, who was twenty-four. "At 6.30 Mary came to my room to announce to me her engagement," Queen Mary noted in her diary. "We were very cheerful and almost uproarious at dinner. We are delighted." Four months later, the wedding in Westminster Abbey was the first state pageant of the peace and one of the last in which Queen Alexandra appeared.

With the needs of her sister and other relatives making demands on her purse, the dowager Queen decided at last on a policy of retrenchment. She was experiencing difficulty with her sight and the resolve to close Marlborough House and live permanently at Sandringham entailed no hardship.

The Queen's notions of household expenditure were however haphazard. At dinner one night Princess Victoria spilt her wine and the Queen scolded her, "The laundry is very expensive!" At this moment, the Empress Marie, trying to reach some toast, upset her own glass. "This is terrible! We shall all be ruined!" the Queen cried. But there was so much laughter that the Queen joined in and gently turned her own glass over.

In January 1923, the Duke of York telegraphed to York Cottage from St. Paul's Walden Bury signalling his own engagement, and on January 20th the Lady Elizabeth Bowes-Lyon first came to Sandringham to meet her prospective parents-in-law and Queen Alexandra.

It was an ordeal that only the charming Lady Elizabeth (the late Queen Mother) could have faced with equanimity: the oddity of York Cottage itself compared with the classic distinction of her own Georgian home; Queen Mary's searching eyes; the hoarse bluffness of the King, who had dreaded the thought of a daughter-in-law and immediately found himself disarmed. Above all, the meeting with the tiny mummified figure at the Big House, deaf, half-blind, her wig too large, rings chinking on her bony fingers, perhaps clinging to her with some remote tale of "Eddy".

But Lady Elizabeth also saw, as T. E. Lawrence did, "the ghosts of all her loving airs, the little graces ... the famous smile, all angular and heart-rending..." There was an added poignancy in the meeting of the twenty-three-year-old young woman who would one day preside at Sandringham as châtelaine and the old lady for whom the house had been built in the long ago. And there was compassion.

The King and Queen now saw Queen Alexandra only when they were at Sandringham, often not for nine months at a time. Queen Mary's diaries on these occasions are occupied chiefly with York Cottage "which looked very nice" or going to tea with Mama "she looked well in the face but it is difficult to understand what she says".

King George, too, would contentedly note "Our dear Cottage is as comfortable as ever". He does not appear to have blamed Sandringham for the toll of coughs, colds and rheumatism, though his severe bronchial attack in 1925 clearly followed on a cold that developed there.

Queen Alexandra celebrated her eightieth birthday in December 1924, a pleasant family occasion with a programme of films in the ballroom: Rudolph Valentino in *Monsieur Beaucaire* and a film of events in her own life, crowded with frisky Coronation horses and the endless rides of the Rose Days, which the public loved and the Queen detested.

What she made of it all is hard to say. "I feel completely collapsed — I shall soon go", one finds her writing to her son three or four months later and, among her few visitors now, her nephew, Prince Nicholas, noticed her pathetic "flashes of remembrance".

Queen Alexandra suffered a fatal heart attack on November 19th 1925, and died the following day. For five days her body rested in Sandringham Church before the altar of solid silver — and, some say, of solid ugliness — that Rodman Wanamaker had presented in commemoration of her husband fourteen years before.

Once again the men of the estate kept their watch, the candlelight glinting about them on the memorial to the Duke of Clarence, on the tablets to estate policemen and bailiffs, on the silver cross that Alexandra had herself placed in the church in memory of the men of the estate who had died in the war.

We can imagine the smoke of the tapers rising towards the roof of painted oak that had been given by King George in thankfulness for a world restored. Outside, during the vigil, there was an early snowfall. And presently the gun-carriage moves away, past the frosted rhododendrons and firs, finally down the hill towards Wolferton Station.

10: THE NEW TENANTS

I

George and Mary had lived at York Cottage for over fifteen years as King and Queen and for more than thirty years of marriage. "Our dear old home... I am sad at leaving it with its many memories and old associations," the Queen wrote to her husband, in the autumn of 1926 after enjoying the beauty of a rare Sandringham summer, but she turned with relish to the task of making the atmosphere of the Big House her own.

A general stocktaking of the immense country house had begun in January. "Such a bewildering lot of things and pictures," was Queen Mary's first impression, now that she could study it all with a more intent eye. Nearly every square inch of embossed wall was indeed covered by oil paintings, photographs or watercolours, shields or rotting trophies of the chase and decrepit weapons of half-forgotten African battles.

Lithographs of Disraeli still hung over the corner fireplace in the office-room under the stairs. A box on the wall was still filled with obsolete telegraph forms that the maids sedulously dusted day after day. Nothing seemed to have been thrown away in sixty years. There were "odds and ends which beloved Mama would poke into every corner of the house, which was such a pity". The Queen also sharply noted that curtains and carpets and wallpapers had faded, but "one would have to make do". There would be marks on the walls when anything was moved but all the pictures — and almost everything else — wanted sorting out and rearranging.

Queen Mary chiefly dedicated herself to this task of rehabilitation, as we see, in the summer. She was then fifty-nine years of age. Walking vigorously past the lakes and up the slope to the House she was enraptured at the flowerbeds and the smooth freshness of the lawns. Ivy had been allowed to encroach on the façades; the Queen ordered it to be cut away. It would be pleasant, she decided, for a wistaria to be encouraged against the billiard room, over Teulon's brickwork.

The Prince of Wales came down to see the alterations and, the Queen reported, "He was simply enchanted with Sandringham in the summer and with the lovely flowerbeds in front of the house. I don't think he had ever been here in the summer since he was a child."

The King and Queen pondered whether they could fit a regular summer visit into their schedules. Princess Victoria was installed at Coppins, and Miss Knollys was given a flat in London where she was to survive into her nineties, but the idea of a summer reunion had its appeal.

Meanwhile, the Queen was immersed in her "alterations". The domestic staff was occupied for days, carrying every doubtful object into the ballroom, which became a vast warehouse of Edwardiana. "Hope you are gradually getting the ballroom cleared" the King chided. "I do not want it to become a store room or lumber room."

By the end of August the Queen could pace unimpeded through rooms cleared of bric-a-brac and airy and bright. Pictures had been "matched up" and no doubt, as Prince Christopher found at Buckingham Palace, she decorated some of the personal rooms with new freshness and simplicity, "perfect in the colour scheme and the furniture chosen to harmonise".

Queen Mary's lady-in-waiting, Lady Bertha Dawkins, declared that some of the rooms, formerly so overcrowded and overloaded with trifles, would not be recognised. Hidden among the junk there were in fact still some good pieces of furniture which had but to be effectively displayed or exposed to the eye to seem transformed. Some of it, decent early nineteenth-century stuff, had been acquired from Spencer Cowper and perhaps through him from Palmerston. A few eighteenth-century pieces may have been brought from Beachamwell. The general effect was of a fastidious taste imposed on the old, as mahogany and lacquered furniture were marshalled with cabinets of Sandringham miniatures, and Chinese porcelains.

"At last I can report everything is now as nice as I can make it," the Queen eventually wrote. Nor could she refrain from mentioning that Annie Jones, the schoolmaster's wife, had been enchanted and had complimented her by saying, "You have made alterations without altering the character of Sandringham."

"And I think this is true," Queen Mary added, with pride.

The King and Queen took up residence on October 14th 1926. By the happiest chance there was a baby in the house at least briefly during their first Christmas season, for the Duke and Duchess of York motored over for a day from St. Paul's Walden Bury, bringing their little daughter, the eight-month-old Princess Elizabeth (now Her Majesty Queen Elizabeth II). This fittingly inaugurated the new family atmosphere of the renovated mansion.

The Prince of Wales, Prince Henry (Duke of Gloucester) the twenty-four-year-old Prince George (the former Duke of Kent) and their friends helped to fill the rooms of the bachelor wing above the library. In the course of time many new friends came on the Sandringham scene such as Lord Eldon, Lord Sefton, Lord Airlie and the Dukes of Norfolk and Beaufort, but the routine varied little through the next nine years.

The King departed as little as possible from what had been done in the old days. The immemorial Sunday afternoon walk continued as usual after the roast beef luncheon, though now the King liked to visit his budgerigars and the rare birds "from the Empire" that shared the aviary. The racing pigeons became prominent, in the care of Walter Jones. The King's racing fortunes were reviving and, indeed, in 1928, his bay filly, Scuttle, won the One Thousand Guineas, the King's only classic victory.

A stud was reorganised at Hampton Court but the best mares remained at Sandringham, under the care of Eddy Walker. One of the great characters of the estate, Walker had begun at Sandringham as stud groom in 1887 and seemed to embody tradition even more than the King. He still held his post, indeed, in 1937 in the reign of King George VI. And then there was the cautious and pessimistic Bland, the head keeper, who would invariably be summoned as soon as the King arrived from London and face his employer's banter, "Well, Bland, all the partridges drowned, I suppose?"

King Edward VII for all his common touch had always been dominantly the monarch before he was the squire. King George V when in Norfolk always succeeded in becoming squire of Sandringham rather than its king. Sandringham had been his predominant childhood setting with "the dogs at the kennels and the bear and the hawk and the hens". His boyish memories were of "dear old Sandringham, just the same", with archery and stump cricket, rabbiting with the keepers, fishing or rambling the marshes with Mr. Jones. If they saw a rare waterbird, Jones would insist on getting out the bird books afterwards to discover its identity, and in George V's earliest shooting days, as we have seen, George Brereton, an admired friend eight years his senior, had taught him the attractions of the teal and snipe and erratic woodcock.

The affairs at the farm also were matters of personal consequence and pride. George Brereton, among others, had taught the King the elements of farming and stockbreeding and in early manhood he took over one of the smaller estate farms and ran it punctiliously as his own. (The wedding gifts on his marriage had included a cow.)

On succeeding to the throne, he felt that the royal farms should set an example: he bought the best stock to strengthen his herds and expected the best results. In the mid-nineteen-twenties, for example, the King paid the top price for the best two-year-old heifer of the Red Poll society's show at Ipswich. The bull Royal Crimson was twice reserve champion at the Royal Shows and in ensuing years the Sandringham herd provided winners in the yearling heifer, two-year-old heifer and young cow classes.

The stud of Sandringham Shire horses was similarly judicious in purchases and successful in championships. At the kennels the King introduced Black Labradors which he had long been breeding. Of one of the dogs, Sandringham Scrum, he remarked with pride that if the dog failed to pick up game, no other dog could find it. A famous Clumber, Sandringham Spark, also regularly won firsts at Crufts, and the King was satisfied that Sandringham enjoyed due prestige as a sporting kennels.

The King succeeded, in fact, in establishing the composite aura of manager and father inherent in a country squire. By purchases that were not always judicious, his domain had now been built up to 20,000 acres and, riding round some small corner of this vast estate the small bearded figure would doff his hat gravely on passing a woman cottager and bid her

"Good morning" in a voice that could be heard on the other side of a copse. Dismounting in West Newton, he not infrequently called on his tenants and "he always wiped his feet, the King did, he never forgot, not he".

The Sandringham clocks were still kept half an hour fast. Punctual to the second by their time, the King appeared at breakfast, with his pet parrot, Charlotte, on his finger. The parrot enjoyed the freedom of the table, and picked and pecked her way among the breakfast things, to the joy of young grandchildren.

Afterwards there came the anxious consideration of the weather if shooting was proposed. The big days were rarer, the hand-reared birds fewer, but the luncheon tent would still be set up in a field, punctiliously carpeted with straw and, after the morning's bag was counted, the approach of gamekeeper Bland to the King's side was, as the Duke of Windsor has testified "as solemn and grave as that of an ambassador presenting his letters of credence".

Before dinner, "Household" and visitors assembled in the drawing-room; and the meal was always graced with the formality of evening dress and decorations, the Queen with diamonds in her hair. The service was, as ever, so swift and effective that guests were often astonished at the shortness of the meal. When Queen Mary rose, it was the signal for the ladies to follow her out, each curtseying to the King and receiving a bow in return.

Afterwards, in the library or drawing-room, the King enjoyed listening to old favourites on the gramophone and never needed persuasion to a game of poker. It was a simple, elegant, unostentatious life, but this well-ordered existence was to be broken by recurrent illness.

Indeed, King George V had been occupant of Sandringham House for barely two years when, after a week's shooting with a house party in particularly cold November weather in 1928, he returned to London and retired to bed complaining of a feverish chill.

It was worse than he knew; the doctors had to operate for an infection at the base of the right lung and the King's wavering temperature caused great concern. "Papa has damaged the valves of his heart, probably overdoing the shooting," the Queen wrote, in urgently recalling the Prince of Wales from East Africa. This was intended to be peremptory but reassuring: actually, the King hovered between life and death.

It was January before he could talk of convalescence at Sandringham and this prospect alarmed the doctors: they advocated milder seaside air, a house was leased near Bognor, and it was not until August 1929 that the doctors allowed him to leave "at *last* for Sandringham", as Queen Mary wrote "delighted to be home again. Everything looked delightful."

With emotion inspired by the ordeal through which the Sovereign had passed, large crowds greeted him at Wolferton and lined the roads to the house. The King saluted them gravely and walked about that same day in his garden, until the rain drove him in. The doctors and nurses watched him with care. He walked a little each day, full of pleasure at once more seeing his horses, his dogs and birds.

A lift had been installed to save him the strain of walking upstairs, but three weeks elapsed before he was allowed to stay downstairs for dinner. Two weeks more, and he mounted a pony, with an equerry walking beside him. Another two weeks and he went out with his new 20-bore guns, killing a dozen pheasants, though he was glumly forced to confide to his diary, "I did not distinguish myself." The expedition resulted, however, from having practised steadily, lifting his gun indoors: after this he could shoot a little whenever it pleased him.

Unfortunately pain from neuritis still intermittently plagued the King; at Sandringham, in April 1930, he caught another feverish cold, and so it went on. But he began spending more time at Sandringham, as if with some inner sense that the scene was closing in. He went there to await the outcome of the General Election in August 1931, when in the face of the severe economic blizzard an all-Party national administration was formed.

He returned to Sandringham that year after the opening of Parliament and the King's more frequent visits had the effect of giving his country home a firmer place in national sentiment. But he caught his usual cold before Christmas again and had to keep to his rooms as the New Year approached and listen enviously to the crack of the guns in the coverts.

In 1932, however, there came an innovation that placed Sandringham House in contact with half the world and brought the King's bluff, paternal presence vividly before millions of his peoples.

II

King George V's voice had been broadcast as early as April 1924, when he opened the British Empire Exhibition at Wembley. His inaugural speech at the Naval Conference in 1930 had been heard by short-wave radio in New Zealand, and beamed by telephone to North America, Australia and Japan. Although India had received only a "brassy roaring" and other failures were reported, the experiment was renewed with the opening of the India Conference in 1931.

Queen Mary noted the improving success of these ventures and, unwilling herself to use the Sandringham telephone, she surprisingly foresaw the advantage to the monarchy of a direct and informal contact between the King and his subjects. Lord Reith first suggested a royal broadcast, in the form of a Christmas message from the Savoy Hill studios in 1927, but it is doubtful if the project reached the ears of the King. The idea was revived and the prospects of a broadcast from the Savoy Hill studios were discussed between Lord Reith as B.B.C. Director-General, Lord Stamfordham and the Archbishop of Canterbury in 1929. But the King could not entirely divorce "the wireless" from the chattering of comedians that came to him on the loudspeaker in his Sandringham sitting-room.

A visit with the Queen to the new-built Broadcasting House in 1932 showed him the new status of broadcasting and the Duke of Windsor has told us how Queen Mary now exerted her own influence in persuasion. Still with misgivings, the King gave in without enthusiasm, and agreed to broadcast at Christmas that year.

"It was not easy," he afterwards told Archbishop Lang, "to find some simple words which everyone could understand, spoken in one and a half minutes. Anyhow, they came from my heart and if they were appreciated I am happy."

Behind the scenes the B.B.C. and Post Office engineers visited Sandringham to scheme and test the landline some three months beforehand. The King's voice was to be carried by local telephone to Wolferton where the circuit joined the main trunk lines along the railway to King's Lynn before being carried by three lines simultaneously to London.

When this layout was explained to Queen Mary, she unerringly noticed an unavoidable weak spot as the line crossed a road to the Lynn exchange. "If a motorcar should hit a telephone pole just there," she enquired, "what would happen?"

The engineers could not reassure her, though they fussed a good deal to make their plans as foolproof as could be. Twenty-four crates of amplifiers entered Sandringham and it is said that an emergency sound circuit was looped north via Sheffield. Lord Knollys' old office off the hall, which the King normally never entered, was to be used as a studio and two microphones in wooden cabinets on a small table padded by a thick tablecloth were to ensure the "perfect balance" of his voice. The adjoining page's room was used as a control room.

Intensely nervous beforehand, the King had no sooner sat down alone in the wicker-seated chair than the wicker broke and his first words — which were not broadcast — were "God bless my soul!" A light had been fixed to flash a signal to begin, but the King preferred the producer to put his head round the door and raise a hand. The broadcast was essentially of a homely nature. The King first paid tribute to the wonders of science that made his message possible and then went on, "I speak now from my home and my heart to you all; to men and women so cut off by the snows, the desert or the sea that only voices out of the air can reach them; to those cut off from fuller life by blindness, sickness or infirmity, and to those who are celebrating this day with their children and their grandchildren — to all, to each, I wish a happy Christmas. God bless you."

In his own journal the King made the brief entry "At 3.35 I broadcasted a short message of 251 words to the whole Empire from Francis' room". But the broadcast had caught every heart with emotion and Lord Reith termed it, "the most spectacular success in B.B.C. history thus far".

In succeeding years, the emotional impact of that slow hoarse voice did not diminish. In suburban homes and at tables on the other side of the world, family dinner parties would rise to their feet or keep tense silence for the King. Custom had not staled, and the mimic or mocker did not dare to lessen the effect. In the then prevalent picture of the British family of nations the simple Christmas message was a potent, moving and unifying influence.

The King used to complain that the broadcasts spoilt his Christmas Day. "It is rather an effort to me," he confessed to Archbishop Lang. Nevertheless, he took a secret pride in the preparation and delivery and on returning to his family in the saloon he asked how he had sounded. His voice would be heard in rehearsals a day or two beforehand and the family knew, of course, what would be said.

One Christmas his sons went for a stroll and did not return, to the King's annoyance. The Prince of Wales heard of this some months later on asking his father what he thought of a radio talk he had given. "I did not hear it," said the King. "Why should I? You did not listen to mine at Christmas."

From 1933 onwards Archbishop Lang also helped him in his choice of words. The King knew what he wanted to say, but could not precisely get the effect. This was acknowledged in a letter after the Christmas broadcast of 1935 which, curiously, was to prove his last. "From the bottom of my heart I thank you all for the trouble you took about the Christmas Day message. Everyone said it was the best I have done yet."

III

King George V commemorated the twenty-fifth year of his reign by building some jubilee cottages in the estate village of West Newton. Building cottages for the tenantry had been

202

Sandringham's signposts in the landscape of time ever since the building of Louise Cottages to celebrate the birth of King George's eldest sister in 1867, a group enlarged in the year of his own accession. His Coronation year had also been marked by the provision of attractive place signs of carved and painted wood in some of the villages of his domain, a combat with an unalarming wolf being represented, for instance, at Wolferton; the jousting knight, Thomas de Shernbourne, was depicted in lively gallop at Shernborne, while St. Felix sailed a painted sea to Flitcham, the village named after him.

King George returned to Sandringham just after celebrating his seventieth birthday: he had perhaps hoped to enjoy the anniversary in his own home but the resignation, owing to ill-health, of the Prime Minister, Mr. Ramsay MacDonald, and the appointment of Mr. Baldwin as the new premier detained him in London.

The King had reached the age when many old friends were passing from the scene. Lord Stamfordham, Sir Charles Cust, Sir Frederick Ponsonby; the shocks intensified until he presently mourned his favourite sister, Princess Victoria, whose loss was to prove the hardest blow of all.

His partial solace was to ride his estate on his white pony, Jock, inspecting the woods and farms and stables, visiting the newest cottages. Friends found that when walking he had to pause for breath every hundred yards. On one of his last days with a gun, in company with George Brereton, he tired rapidly. "Well, Mr. Brereton, I think I must go home." "Yes sir, we've had a nice morning's sport."

Sandringham was bitterly cold during the Christmas of 1935, and the shadow of Princess Victoria's passing, three weeks before, hung over the company. On Christmas Eve the family gave one another their presents, innocently the two little

Princesses, Lilibet and Margaret, romped around the tree, and the staff received their gifts on Christmas Day.

On New Year's Eve the household gathered in the ballroom for the film of *Monte Cristo* but the King dozed off towards the end, as he was apt to do. He preferred to sit before the fire in his bedroom, clad in his old Tibetan dressing-gown for extra warmth, reading or dozing.

Some newly-appointed ministers came from London to receive their seals of office, among them young Anthony Eden as Foreign Minister, but King George's world was shrinking faster than anyone knew to the fireplace, the armchair, the glimpse from his bay window in the tower, of Sandringham Church rising above the leafless trees, and the brass bedstead that had been his father's. With snow powdering the shrubs and garden beds, the King went out on his pony once or twice in early January, Queen Mary or Princess Elizabeth walking beside him.

There were a fair number of people in the house, among them the Duke of York — the Duchess was ill in London — Lady Desborough, Major Hardinge and Alan Lascelles, and no one dreamed what was impending. On January 14th the King went out of doors for the last time, riding on Jock towards the church and rewarding him as usual with a carrot.

Indoors, Queen Mary was rearranging Queen Alexandra's collection of Fabergé treasures, placing them in the vitrines in which they had originally been displayed. The King enjoyed helping her, recalling some of the occasions when the bibelots had first been given to his mother. He had looked forward to the showing of a Tom Walls comedy film which had been arranged for the 17th. The picture was shown but the King did not feel well enough to come down and watch it. Instead the Prince of Wales "proposed himself", taking his mother's hint that he should pay a visit, and arrived by aeroplane, first circling low around the estate and landing nearby. The sound of aircraft was unusual then at Sandringham. Did the King drowsily recall the Zeppelin he had heard by night twenty-one years before, droning above the woods?

Many elder news correspondents will remember the first bulletin with its anxiety at cardiac weakness; the frantic dash to Sandringham, the scramble for rooms in the inn at Dersingham, the famine of telephones, the picket at every gate of the estate. "Too heartless," Queen Mary recorded it. But a beloved King was known to be dying.

The reporters waited in frost and rain, by day and night, watching the lights of the house. With the arrival of the Archbishop of Canterbury, the coming and going of members of the Royal Family, and the arrival on the Monday of five members of the Privy Council, the vigil was that of the whole world. The story, familiar to an older generation, is still one of tragic drama.

Early that morning the King saw his private secretary, Lord Wigram, for a few moments, and feebly whispered in interrogation the word "Empire?" Lord Wigram answered, "It is all absolutely right, sir." Later that morning the Privy Counsellors were ushered upstairs and found the King propped in his chair with a bed-table across the arms. The purpose of the Council was to appoint Counsellors of State to transact the King's business.

The dying King managed to say "I approve" but found difficulty in signing the Order. His physician, Lord Dawson of Penn, kneeling at his side, suggested he should use his left hand. "Why?" enquired the King, with a flash of humour. "Do you wish me to sign with both hands?"

He would not allow a subject to guide his hand. He would not give up. As he strove with the pen, and it turned weakly between his fingers, he glanced towards his Counsellors, "I am sorry to keep you waiting, gentlemen," he said, and presently achieved two barely recognisable crosses and then dismissed his visitors with a smile. There were tears in their eyes as they came downstairs.

Of the later events of the day, the Archbishop entered in his diary, "We all (the Queen, the Prince of Wales and the rest of the Royal Family) had met at tea — the Prince full of vitality and talk and lovingly attentive to the Queen". The Royal Family dined alone but sent to the Household dining-room for the wording of the nine o'clock bulletin. Lord Dawson of Penn consulted with Lord Wigram and murmured "I think the time is past for details". Then on the back of a menu card he wrote the words, "The King's life is moving peacefully towards its close". The phrase was repeated at intervals in every home that night, by radio, like the tolling of a bell.

At five minutes before midnight the end came. Nor had midnight passed before Queen Mary turned to the new King and, as he wrote years later, "My mother did an unexpected thing. She took my hand in hers and kissed it; before I could stop him, my brother George, who was standing beside her, stepped forward and followed her example."

III

The new King Edward VIII left Sandringham next morning by aeroplane. Nothing so sharply disclosed the changes that must come, for the old King had never flown in his life, and the new King did not realise he was creating a precedent.

King George V's coffin, it was decreed, should be made of oak from a tree felled on the estate, and like his mother's it rested for a time in Sandringham Church. The last journey of all began to the sound of a bagpipe lament as, leading the late King's pony, grooms and gaitered keepers and tenants and neighbours walked in the procession down the hill. And so once again the estate was left, not empty nor silent, but with only its ordinary working population, in the grip of winter.

Before leaving for London, the new King Edward VIII had ordered that all the Sandringham clocks should be returned to standard time. So at long last changes were coming, and the tenants discussed the future with anxiety. Their surmises grew wilder when it became known, in February, that the Duke of York was touring the estate with a stranger and that both were asking many searching questions.

The inquisition — at the farms, the timber mills, the pheasantries, the estate office — went on for a fortnight. The stranger was in fact the Earl of Radnor, a mutual friend of the King and the Duke of York, to whom he was only four days junior, an admirable consultant who had for four years supervised the mining rights and other estate matters of the Duchy of Cornwall and successfully managed large estates of his own.

The new King had long felt that Sandringham was a white elephant, a Rip Van Winkle wonderland, that caused a continuous and to his mind prodigal drain on private royal funds. Edward and his brother had already realised in their father's lifetime, in fact, that reforms were overdue. Game birds, for instance, were still being raised on too vast a scale, the flax experiment at the farm had begun to lose money and the Privy Purse had been an ever-open granary to make up losses.

The Duke of York was of the opinion that the estate could pay its way if running expenses could be reduced under sensible modern management, and the survey, affording him access for the first time to the accounts, seemed to confirm his point of view.

As his father had done, the Duke preferred the Sandringham tenants to be the Sandringham workpeople but this benevolent oligarchy was clearly no longer possible. Many of the innumerable farms that had been acquired were found to have suffered from the lack of individual management and responsibility. Father to son, ever enlarging families had been blithely getting "jobs for the boys" until the estate was over-burdened with labour. Charged with the task of enquiring into the means of reform, the Duke had to sink personal considerations and he put forward a report which the King called "excellent".

The King's farming was to be restricted to twelve hundred acres, including the rearing of pedigree cattle at Wolferton and Appleton, but the farms at Anmer and more outlying regions were otherwise to be let to the tenants, and workpeople transferred to their employment were to receive a parting bonus.

It seems, however, that the King had mental reservations, for when he effected changes of personnel and establishment at Balmoral later in the year, the Duke of York was not consulted, although he was readily available at Birkhall. We are told by his biographer that the Duke was pained at thus being ignored.

Another unhappy sequel to the reorganisation was the resignation of Mr. Edmund Beck, "the last of the Becks" as land agent. It is strange that their family regime, which had lasted over a hundred years, should have ended under a landlord who, as King, was at Sandringham only once and for only a day. This was at the time when Mrs. Simpson, the lady whom he married after relinquishing the throne, rented a house at Felixstowe as a preliminary to the hearing of her divorce petition at the Ipswich assizes on October 27th.

On Sunday, October 18th, the King arrived intending to enjoy four days' partridge shooting with a few friends while at the same time bidding farewell to the scores of departing employees. The members of the small shooting party included Sir Samuel Hoare, the Earl of Harewood, a Mr. H. A. Brown and Sir Humphrey de Trafford. But the King was only out for a few hours with the guns when, with some secrecy, he returned to his home at Fort Belvedere for what turned out to be the first of the salient talks with his Prime Minister, Mr. Baldwin, the talks that within eight weeks led to the Abdication.

The only other phase of residence of King Edward VIII's brief reign concerned not the King himself, but Queen Mary, who came in August to spend a month or more, after sadly relinquishing her rooms in Buckingham Palace. "I am glad to be here," she confided to the privacy of her diary, "but miss my G. too dreadfully, his rooms look so empty and deserted."

She had forced herself to enter her husband's closed suite, and the whole house was thick-clustered with recollections, the sad time "when Grannie became so frail", as she wrote to her son. But there were also "so many happy memories of my whole married life… Papa adored this place and I love it".

Her letter to the King suggests some fuller permanence, as if she had intended to make her home at Sandringham, "It is very nice here and peaceful and I am sure I shall like it". The contents of royal wills are not divulged but it would appear that King George V followed his father's example in leaving the Big House as a dower-house to his widow while the estate passed to his eldest son.

Since Queen Mary outlived him, it appears that King George VI was never an unrestricted landlord, and enjoyed Sandringham itself subject to his mother's tenancy. The financial terms under which King George VI or his daughter took over the estate have remained private. In 1937, however, it was with a sense of liberation that Queen Mary and the Royal Family returned to Sandringham after the turmoil of the Abdication had passed.

"Left London with Bertie, E. and their children for dear Sandringham to spend Christmas, my staff running it this year" she wrote. "Happy to be back in the old Home." And the entire nation felt a sense of relief at the presence of the Royal Family at Sandringham after the months of dissension and strain.

The King had gone, but the King had come home, and at the root of the renewed Sandringham Christmas was an assurance of the continuity of tradition and the goodness of family life that is the modern strength of the monarchy.

11: THE YOUNG FAMILY

The onset of the Coronation Year of 1937 found a new atmosphere at Sandringham House, for it was some sixty years since there had been so small and youthful a family group in residence.

King George VI was only a year within the gate of his forties, his consort Queen Elizabeth (the late Queen Mother) was not then thirty-seven. Their two little daughters, Princess Elizabeth and Princess Margaret, walking hand in hand to visit the stables, were in their eleventh and seventh years.

In one old coach-house, some extraordinary equipages of interest to the children were still to be found, a Japanese rickshaw, two ancient Norwegian carioles, the Hungarian victoria from Budapest and an immense padded charabanc that had belonged to the Emperor Napoleon III. A saddle-room contained treasures sometimes meaningful but often mysterious to Princess Elizabeth, splendid sets of Indian harness, Fred Archer's racing saddle and a Mexican saddle with lasso attached that had been presented to Buffalo Bill.

The children sometimes ran home eagerly to report their discoveries. The present Queen remembered the curiosities she had first seen in childhood — the stuffed head of Persimmon, the bicycle on which her grandfather had learned to ride, the Union Jack found near the body of Captain Scott in the Antarctic — and directed that they should be put on show during a Sandringham fete.

The "new deal" of the estate reorganisation subtly accentuated the simple and close-knit intimacy of the fresh family group. The management of the farms passed appropriately into the hands of Mr. Mackinnon, who for ten years had managed the farms of St. Paul's Walden Bury, the new Queen Consort's family home.

It seemed in keeping that Captain W. A. Fellowes, similarly, was only thirty-seven years old; and in his fresh appointment as land agent, with ample mature timber coming into yield, he had begun a vigorous programme of afforestation which was to see new saplings planted over ten per cent of the estate.

As the new King and Queen took their first walks of family proprietorship around Sandringham House, they trod new-planted lawns. The time had come to replace the finicky flowerbeds of the western garden, involving the labour of five men most of the week, with greensward which could be trimmed by a man and a machine in a day. The Queen, too, had early decided that her Coronation gift to her husband should take the family form of a group of houses in the estate village. Built in brick and carstone, single-storied and designed for elderly couples, her cottages, in fact, filled a need.

Visiting the new site, the King noticed that the occupant of another cottage had filled in the space between his back door and store shed with a glazed roof and French doors, creating a loggia of pleasant aspect.

The idea was mentally pigeonholed and copied a decade later when a crescent of Victory Cottages contributed their mite to the shortage of post-war housing. Although these were built by the Clerk of the Works department, the royal couple gave considerable thought and care both to the siting and the finish. Thus the bow windows were an element included at the King's special order and the painted deal chimney-pieces of simple Regency pattern were chosen by the King and Queen as part of their own quota of patronage of good design.

Probably the close watch on detail took up too much of the King's time and energy. As his biographer, Sir John Wheeler-Bennett, has said, "No addition could be made to a cottage, no new tenant taken on, no employee discharged, no tree cut down, without the King's approval". Every decision was submitted to him personally, even when he was in London, and he regarded estate correspondence as so highly personal that he invariably replied in his own hand.

At the Big House Queen Mary and her daughter-in-law had the felicity of perfect agreement on the now overdue redecoration. There was much recarpeting. The saloon was rejuvenated by being decorated throughout in pastel ivory. The high-polished Victorian parquetry panelling that had for so long imparted a heavy and frowning atmosphere to the dining-room was stripped away, and the Spanish tapestries sympathetically and freshly enhanced with palest green.

Queen Mary returned to enjoy these novelties in the August of Coronation year and felt so much younger that, at seventy, she enjoyed herself thoroughly at a ball at Houghton Hall, taking part in the waltzes.

The simplicity of the new reign is also echoed in the Sandringham game books. The King indeed brought a new book into use especially to record the duck shooting and give him ready comparisons of the results at different ponds from year to year.

King George VI was the kind of sportsman who rose before six a.m. to wait alone for the morning flight. Alone one morning in October 1937, at Frankfort Pool, he watched a cloud of 150 teal streaming over and recorded his bag of forty-eight mallard with satisfaction. He had shot sixty-nine mallard with Captain Fellowes at Wolferton Splash the previous evening and noticed that he and his partner were too close together. "A one-gun place" he summarised.

The same fault was observed three or four days later when six guns were distributed over Wolferton Creek, Frankfort and Park Ponds and 111 mallard and thirteen teal were obtained.

A great tidying of all the watersides went on at this time, reeds and weed being cut where necessary, fresh platforms prepared for the duck, reed screens and shooting tubs placed for use in alternative winds. But the King wanted to be constantly informed what species were coming in, and to encourage recognition among his staff large coloured illustrations of the different ducks were hung in the estate office and deployed wherever Alfred Amos, who was now head keeper, could find useful wall space.

With careful records established, the King did not spoil his pools by seeking the same site too soon. Having decided that Wolferton Splash was a one-gun place, he did not return until four weeks later. Then he was alone in the November dusk, the duck came steadily in and he secured eighty mallard and a pintail. Incidentally, this was the pool first excavated by the Zeppelin bomb in 1915, an ideal evening flight pool after being broadened, with a sluice to control the fresh water.

Back in London, the monarch would receive the report "There are plenty of duck in now" and had to resist temptation. In those few fleeting pre-war years there was too much business to permit impromptu visits to Norfolk.

The rush of Coronation year, the tension of political events, the recurrent crises of Hitler's aggressions in Europe, the State Royal Visit to France and the plans for a visit to Canada and the United States, all these happenings, pressing and absorbing, nevertheless heightened the serenity of the Sandringham winter scene when the Royal Family could at last relax there.

The King had not yet broadcast from Sandringham, thinking modestly — and mistakenly — that the success of the Christmas talks was personal to his father. In 1937, however, he felt that a message of gratitude was due to the peoples who had acclaimed his Coronation and he pretended to make light of the stammer that made the broadcast and preliminary rehearsals an intense ordeal.

He refused to permit a pre-recording to be made as a safety measure. "I want my people to hear *my* voice," he told the sound engineers, "not what you think should be my voice." Lionel Logue, his speech consultant, came down from London to be at his side and advise that the King should speak standing, since a sitting position inhibits correct rhythm and breathing.

Listening to the King's voice during the tense and hesitant rehearsals, the engineers were so doubtful that they declined champagne with their own Christmas dinner in the Steward's Room before the broadcast, lest the wine should impair their efficiency. (They had discovered on an earlier occasion the strength of royal port.)

In reality, the only contretemps occurred after the broadcast, when the King immediately went into the control room to hear the playback. His jubilant Queen and the two Princesses joined him, the London engineers were still talking by telephone to their Sandringham colleagues and the replaying of the National Anthem suddenly froze the Royal Family and engineers to attention. London, of course, did not know what was happening and from the telephones came plaintive squeaks, "Sandringham! Sandringham! Why don't you answer?"

II

Queen Mary, that constant commentator, noted the pleasant

overture to 1938, when the Garbo film *Marie Walewska* was shown in the ballroom. "At midnight sang *Auld Lang Syne* and had a snap dragon — very nice being all together." But this was the year that brought the annexation of Austria and the false peace of Munich.

The troubled atmosphere seemed to match the crash of trees felled in the distant plantations. There seemed once again to be long periods when the house was deserted and only maids who were accustomed to the lonely silence could work undaunted amid the dust-sheeted shapes of furniture under the blank surveillance of the smiling portraits. The life of rooms and corridors at such times stood in suspense, secretive behind drawn blinds, the stillness broken only by the birdsong across the empty lawns.

With forty and even thirty miles an hour still the motoring speed average, Sandringham still seemed too far for weekends and in any case the King preferred the smaller simplicity of Royal Lodge. But at Christmas Wolferton Station was once more decorated with balloons and holly and the procession of cars and luggage vans again wound up the hill.

At the last Christmas of the pre-war years there were charades and Queen Mary thought it worth mention that "we ladies put on funny hats for dinner" and the soundtrack of *Alexander's Ragtime Band* blared in the ballroom. But 1939 was barely a week old when there were fire-drills and ARP (air-raid precaution) exercises, watched with excitement by the young Princesses craning eagerly from a staircase window. The King was out wildfowling one morning towards the end of his stay. The duck had left the coast and he had shot only one mallard. It was a singularly unlucky bird and almost a bird of ill omen.

On Sunday morning, September 3rd, Mr. Fuller, the rector, had installed his wireless set in the nave of Sandringham

Church to enable his congregation to hear the fateful Chamberlain speech that was to announce war or peace.

Queen Mary was among the worshippers, surrounded by the memorials of royal dead, who listened to the music of *The Flowers That Bloom in the Spring* that with casual absurdity introduced the Prime Minister's solemn voice and was followed by the first mournful wail of the air-raid siren, that famous false alarm.

A more annoying alert occurred in the small hours next morning when the Queen hurriedly had to dress while her detective waited outside the door and then descend with him to the basement. The young Kent children, Edward and Alexandra, then mere toddlers, were carried down, barely waking.

Next morning, Queen Mary set off for Badminton, where she was to stay for the duration of the war, and she seldom visited Norfolk in the next six years. It came as a surprise when the King and Queen and their daughters spent the first war Christmas at Sandringham after all. The house was admittedly exposed to the East Coast visit of German reconnaissance planes but the lull of those early months seemed to justify the element of risk.

Princess Elizabeth found a new pony awaiting her and the children delighted their parents by singing French duets, a surprise prepared in conspiracy with their French teacher.

The King again broadcast that year, the first of the series that continued to his death. A religious man, he spoke with hardly a pause the lines of poetry in which he found faith, "'…put your hand into the Hand of God. That shall be better than light and safer than a known way'. May that Almighty Hand guide and uphold us all" and the phrase was echoed with fervour in newspapers and pulpits.

Sandringham House itself was closed through the remaining five long war years. The lawns around the house were ploughed up to yield oats and rye; the private golf course, where the bunkers had so angered King Edward VII, now finally disappeared under potatoes. Beetroots and parsnips, peas and beans, were grown in the flowerbeds.

The marshes were tilled and on the rarer occasions when the King could enjoy wildfowling it was among lands with a high yield of wheat, oats and mustard. The harvest was achieved chiefly by fourteen girls of the Land Army; and since troops were billeted at York Cottage elements of romance also blossomed.

Meanwhile, the more customary sport of the estate at times contributed unexpected quotas to food supplies. Late in September 1941, for instance, when was activity was mainly confined to the Russian front, the King was pressed to take a few days' leave and a party of six guns was made up by telephone at twenty-four hours' notice.

In the next six days they bagged over 6,200 partridges, as well as pheasants, pigeons, hares and rabbits, a bag all the more remarkable in that the party mostly had to do their own picking up. As Mr. Aubrey Buxton has pointed out, the astonishing total ranked with the record of 4,749 birds achieved at Holkham in four memorable days in 1905, and was certainly a cause of great satisfaction to the King.

Both for economy and security, the Royal Family stayed on these occasions at Appleton House, the renovated Cresswell farmhouse which had been Queen Maud of Norway's winter home. Now the Princesses' bicycles sometimes stood against the wall and Queen Elizabeth's pony and trap was much in evidence.

The Chief of the Imperial General Staff, Field Marshal Sir Alan Brooke, was a guest early in 1943, when the victories of the Western Desert signalled the turning point of the war, and he has left us a picture of the pleasant undercurrent of domesticity: twelve-year-old Princess Margaret laughing to herself over a copy of *Punch*, the Queen pouring tea, the quiet series of talks in the King's study.

Dinner was served at 8.45, the company assembling beforehand in the drawing-room, the men in dress uniform. Afterwards the Queen disguised the shortage of coffee by offering tea, and the sessions of private talk with the King were resumed until eleven-thirty. Although the kitchen of Appleton was operated under a catering licence, food rations were now at their leanest.

Brooke's batman confided to the Field Marshal that the estate grew good Cox's Orange Pippins which were sent to market. "We could bring some home with us?" he suggested, "and I could pay the gardener." Sir Alan Brooke could see no harm in buying the apples, but he felt like a guilty schoolboy when the King came out to speak to his chauffeur as they were leaving. "I had one ghastly moment that he would find the whole of the back of the car packed with his best apples. But Lockwood (the batman) was too clever to be caught out like that: there were lots of them all cleverly hidden, and all had been paid for."

The King was at Appleton for Princess Elizabeth's birthday in 1945 when he heard of the peace overtures from Heinrich Himmler and went at once to London.

III

To be back in the "Big House" for Christmas, to know that the telephone or telegrams or letters would no longer bring tragic news of friends and relatives, to pay no attention to the friendly aircraft roaring overhead from the nearby American bases, to pay no heed to the soft drone of bombers in the night... Sandringham, as every home in Britain, celebrated the inimitable zest of the first post-war Christmas.

The nineteen-year-old elder daughter of the house was in love, always awaiting the postman, and the guests tended to be a younger age group than the King and Queen.

Queen Mary's old lady-in-waiting, Lady Airlie, noticed how much the atmosphere had changed. "In the entrance hall there now stood a baize-covered table on which jigsaw puzzles were set out. The younger members of the party, the Princesses, Mrs. Gibbs (Princess Elizabeth's lady-in-waiting) and several young Guardsmen congregated round them from morning till night. The radio, worked by Princess Elizabeth, blared incessantly."

The King, toiling and overworking at his boxes, was apt to appear only for meals and return to his desk afterwards. Yet the new atmosphere was more friendly and casual. Though the guests assembled as usual in the drawing-room before dinner, orders and medals were conspicuously absent and it was probably only in deference to Queen Mary that the men, if out of uniform, wore white ties.

Late one night dancing began to some old-time music. Nearly in their eighties, Queen Mary and Lady Airlie found they could still dance with spirit in *Hickey Hoo* and *Stripping the Willow*, even the strenuous *Sir Roger de Coverley*, and it was nearly one o'clock before anyone thought of bedtime.

In contrast with this gaiety, a visit was paid to York Cottage, where the dilapidation of military occupation was dismaying. It may have been conjectured at this time whether it could not be put in order for another young royal married couple. The question was perhaps in the air in 1946 when Prince Philip came on leave and spent his first Christmas at Sandringham.

Many houses in lesser plight faced demolition but the sentimental objections to this were strengthened by the need for larger office and living accommodation for the estate staff. Eventually the original house with its reception rooms was converted into the estate office while five flats, each with three bedrooms, were ingeniously contrived in the Edwardian warren of the extension that lay beyond.

In 1947, too, the King and Queen initiated a new garden immediately to the north of the "Big House", alongside the glade watched by Admiral Keppel's Chinese joss. Mr. G. A. Jellicoe, the architect who had sympathetically remodelled the grounds of Royal Lodge, was placed in charge and, as he has said, the King was profoundly influenced by the garden affections of the Queen, which included a penchant for the enclosed Scottish garden.

The proposal was for a secluded garden within the garden, but estate sentiment also entered the King's thoughts, for the garden was to be set within a rectangle of pleached lime walks, reminiscent of the avenue of lime trees on the site once familiar to Mr. Motteux.

Adjoining the King's private rooms at the north end of the house he would now have a sequestered pleasance which he could readily enter and enjoy without being seen from the drive or by anyone crossing the park. In the maturing outcome some might object to a finicky effect in the low box hedges but the King deliberately sought a cosy restraint in contrast with the spacious and sweeping grandeur evident elsewhere.

On the Christmas visit after their honeymoon in 1947, Princess Elizabeth and Prince Philip could stroll among the young standards and immature planting of the embryo garden without being observed from the Wolferton road.

In spite of stringent petrol rationing, crowds, however, scrambled without dignity around the church on Christmas morning to catch a glimpse of the young couple. The same phenomenon, by no means a new one, occurred at West Newton when the Royal Family arrived for the evening service of carols.

These public mêlées aside, the pattern of the post-war Sandringham Christmas was established — the blizzard of Christmas cards settling like snowflakes in every room, the piled gift-tables, the airborne bouquets arriving from the Antipodes.

The meat hand-out to estate employees disappeared with meat rationing, if not earlier, but two hundred Christmas puddings — in a gold giftbox stamped with the royal cipher — were distributed instead. (Sandringham staff cooks were once occupied making plum puddings for all the royal residences for much of the year, but royal Christmas puddings are now purchased in bulk from a London store.)

The house staff, too, received their gifts, as they still do, after tea on Christmas afternoon, assembling in the ballroom corridor, the elder ones wearing their medals of the Royal Victorian Order for long service, the mere calling of their names still observing the formalities of staff precedence and term of service.

Perhaps one should mention here the pleasant custom of sending the Sovereign sprays of the Christmas flowering Holy Thorn from Glastonbury, said to have originally blossomed from the staff of St. Joseph of Arimathea, a custom observed under Charles I and revived during the reign of King George V. Somewhat less assured, I think, is the story that

Sandringham Christmas crackers always have a gift at each end, a speciality provided ever since King George V saw a small boy burst into tears on drawing a blank.

But old customs are forever changing. The estate fire-drills had always been carried out in the monarch's absence but King George VI saw that a more publicised drill might be a useful example in fire prevention and a fuller drill was arranged with the National Fire Service in January 1947.

The King gave the exercise its code word "Crackers" — the name of the Queen's corgi — and the first fire officer to arrive was handed a specific instruction. "A fire has started in the housekeeper's kitchen on the first floor, and is spreading to the housekeeper's staircase and landing. The bachelor wing is also involved. Flames are now visible through the roof above the bachelor wing and the housekeeper's corridor."

Watched in the forecourt by the Royal Family, the exercise included the rescue of two maids by ladder from a window on the second floor, but perhaps the satiric demons that watch human affairs had the last laugh. Outbreaks of fire at Sandringham have been fortunately few, but only four months after the exercise a serious fire occurred in the woodlands and blazed for several days, devastating hundreds of acres.

Prince Philip's name increasingly appears in the Sandringham game books from 1948 onwards. In my book *Prince Philip, Sportsman* I have given some account of his shooting experiences with King George VI but he also received early practical instruction in sporting estate management from his father-in-law.

In wildfowling alone he learned of the landscaping and restraint that kept the flighting pools on a fair sporting level, how the clearance of bushes had given a better view there or a cleaner stretch of water improved results elsewhere.

Ill-health, alas, compelled the King to abandon wildfowling in 1949, and his last expedition, in the early dawn of October 18th, chanced to be in the company of Princess Elizabeth. A party of six guns was stationed elsewhere but the King and his daughter crossed the bridge on to the reed-tipped island of Frankfort Pool and waited for what the dawn would bring. Mallard and teal, widgeon, gadwall, shoveler and pintail were coming in. The role of the Princess was as a watcher only, but when she next visited the island it was in her husband's company.

Another important newcomer also entered on the Sandringham scene in those years, for Prince Charles was taken there for Christmas when five weeks old. (His mother suffered the wry experience of an attack of measles which confined her to her room and separated her from her baby.)

Prince Charles was again in the care of his grandparents at Sandringham for Christmas 1950, when Princess Elizabeth had joined Prince Philip in Malta. "He is too sweet stumping around the room," the King wrote fondly to his daughter. "We shall love having him at Sandringham. He is the fifth generation to live there and I hope he will get to love the place."

The thought, indeed, remained with the King, and as the New Year of 1951 advanced he wrote to Queen Mary in the same vein. "I want Lilibet and Philip to get to know it too as I have always been so happy here and I love the place."

These letters suggest his only inkling of the wind of change. In the summer of the last year of his life he spent a "convalescence" of a summer month at Sandringham, apparently unaware that he was suffering from a malignant carcinoma. After the surgery of the autumn it was a special joy — as it had been with his father — to return for Christmas "so pleased to be back in Norfolk once more", as he wrote to a friend.

The King's broadcast that year was recorded in London beforehand, and the small family party was a particularly carefree and happy one. On leaving his sickbed the invalid had been anxious to learn whether he could still lift a shooting arm, and the discovery that he could do so brightened his eventide of recovery.

The King resumed shooting on New Year's Day, 1952, driving to Heath Farm in his Land Rover with Prince Philip, Lord Dalkeith and others. It was a fine, cold day, the host decided for "cocks only" and the seven guns collected 101 pheasants, four woodcock and sundry hares, rabbits and a pigeon. The King also liked to have a day for pigeons shared with up to a dozen neighbours and tenant farmers, and a drive for rabbits and hares when police and visiting keepers might bring the guns to a score.

Such a day of rural sport was the last of King George VI's life. The bag included 280 hares and the King got three hares with his last three shots. That evening, he planned the next day's sport but did not enter up his game book. He slipped up to the nursery for a few minutes to see Prince Charles and Princess Anne, and afterwards sat, relaxed and contented, listening to a broadcast description of the reception given to Princess Elizabeth and Prince Philip in Kenya.

The story of that last evening scarcely needs retelling and we are concerned only with the chronicle of the house. Yet that night a tiny detail of the fabric was to assume momentous significance. A new fastening had recently been attached to the King's bedroom window and at about midnight a watchman in the garden observed the King affixing the latch. Was it too stubborn for his already overtaxed heart? The King died peacefully in his sleep, ninety years almost to the day since his grandfather had sealed the Sandringham purchase.

12: THE FREEHOLDERS

I

A curious phenomenon was noticed at the main gates of Sandringham shortly after Queen Elizabeth II came to the throne. Visitors stealthily wrenched rosettes and tendrils from the decorative ironwork and in spite of appealing notices and police patrols the vandalism continued in Coronation Year.

The nuisance was akin to the eagerness to touch royalty that once troubled the Duke of Windsor in Canada or to the student mania for stealing hats or car mascots that has annoyed the Duke of Edinburgh; the wishful self-identification with the monarchy that impels onlookers to stare at the blank façade of Buckingham Palace or desperately push and struggle at the gate of Sandringham Church on Christmas Day. Something more than a symptom of quaint loyalty or mere curiosity, it was a ritual of ancient magic, but to the new Queen and her husband this public scrabbling at the gate of their private lives was a manifestation of a deepening problem.

Throughout the twentieth century, as we have seen, Sandringham has provided the Royal Family with its most private residence, its least vulnerable sanctuary, the truest home. Yet early in the 1950's the apparition of the Lynn reporter who had once intruded on Albert Edward while rabbiting was magnified into a feverish, insatiable and world-wide speculation.

Every shooting party was spied upon in the hope of identifying Princess Margaret's suitor, and every estate worker ran a gauntlet of subtle hazards with conversational strangers in the increasingly efficient and intensive fact-finding activities of the press.

The peculiar privacy of Sandringham House was demonstrated in 1952 when the Queen invited Norman Hartnell to lunch to submit the ninth and final design of her Coronation gown and to display dresses, albeit a year ahead, for her 1953–54 Australasian tour.

The collection of dresses entailed two car loads of mannequins and assistants yet the convenience of six separate entrances enabled the party to enter the estate unobserved. After luncheon Mr. Hartnell collected his party together and discovered that his dress show was to be the most informal he had ever presented, for it was to be held in a large bedroom of old-fashioned charm.

The models entered through the large white bathroom adjoining, and the Queen, Queen Elizabeth the Queen Mother and Princess Margaret sat on a slender Victorian sofa at the foot of the enormous bedstead.

After some of the delectable dresses for Australia had been selected — summery confections chosen on a cold and wintry Saturday afternoon — the couturier set out the eleven gilded frames displaying the emblems of the United Kingdom and the Commonwealth which were to be embroidered into the design of the Coronation gown.

The Queen approved all except the Irish Shamrock, which she judged a little too verdant in tone, and then followed the approval of the design for Princess Margaret's dress and the designs for Her Majesty's trainbearers and others.

The Queen at her accession was only twenty-five, her husband thirty years of age, and there is a hint in family records of the shock they experienced in inheriting their responsibilities so soon, almost least among them the onus of the twenty thousand acres and two hundred lives of Sandringham.

Prince Philip toured the house and opened unexplained doors to find what lay beyond. Entering the office where household supplies were managed, he tweaked aside a curtain to see what lay behind it, exposing a table set complete with a bottle of orangeade for an office lunch. In the kitchens, already reasonably modernised under King George VI, the new squire was not satisfied until he knew the precise purpose of the various fittings and equipment.

Noticing the morning delivery of blocks of ice standing on the floor near the kitchen larder, he protested "That won't do at all". Estate carpenters were ordered to make a wooden bench on which the ice could be stacked and two days later the Prince returned to see that his orders had been carried out.

At a garden door a mud-scraper allowed mud to fall on to a porcupine-like brush which lodged some of it back on the boots, and Prince Philip is said to have spent a rainy afternoon designing a new and improved scraper at his drawing-board. After the first introductory tours of the estate with Captain Fellowes, he fell into the habit of going round alone in an estate car, asking questions of anyone he saw on the spot, until workers began to call him "The Gaffer", as they did any foreman.

As his cousin, Queen Alexandra of Yugoslavia, has told us, he passionately wanted to discover not only how the various branches of the estate were run but whether method or results could be improved. The farm manager with a promising new project and gardeners who thought the sixteen acres of kitchen gardens absurdly large for the house found in Prince Philip an unexpected ally.

A friend heard him talking with some excitement one day of Royal Zobo and, knowing the family liking for nicknames, he wondered who Zobo could be. He had heard of Bobo, but not Zobo. She turned out to be a prize-winning Sandringham cow with a record milk yield.

In the first year Prince Philip was content to question and enquire, to register and check. There was an innovation in October when he flew from Balmoral to Sandringham — from Dyce airport to the R.A.F. field at Marsham, King's Lynn — for a week's shooting and back again.

Local airfield resources were more fully utilised early in 1953 when, after his first solo flight, the next stage of his air training was shifted to the nearby R.A.F. station at Bircham Newton.

A new era for Sandringham was notched when the master of the house performed his first solo loop, slow roll and spin, somewhere above the royal estate.

The bush telegraph of the countryside, which always buzzed its news when the Duke was "up", never rang with more excitement and surmise than during his last day in a Chipmunk training plane, practising steep turns and testing for stalling. Even more than King Edward VIII's famous flight, this inaugurated the air age at Sandringham which was to see the Queen flying there in turn from Balmoral and the Queen Mother landing in a helicopter of the Queen's Flight within a few yards of the front door.

The Christmas of Coronation year broke a Sandringham sequence for it was spent, of course, in Auckland, New Zealand, where the Queen received among other gifts a train set that was one day to be a favourite toy on a Sandringham floor. This may indeed have been inaugurated when the Royal Family next gathered at Sandringham for Prince Charles's sixth birthday in 1954, when an improved heating installation was also found in order and much of the house had again been freshly decorated.

With the passing of Queen Mary in 1953, and the willing of certain pieces of her furniture, a rearrangement of furnishing was no doubt discussed with Miss Jessie Robertson, the housekeeper. At Christmas, the presence of the Gloucester and Kent families as well as Princess Margaret and the Queen Mother once again formed a full family house-party and in the Queen's broadcast on sound radio there was evidence enough that she had written her own scripts, perhaps with the solidity of her great-grandfather's house in mind.

"There is nothing quite like the family gathering in familiar surroundings, centred on the children," she said. "When it is night, and the wind and rain beat upon the window, the family is most truly conscious of the warmth and peacefulness that surround the pleasant fireside."

Since then many more Christmases have passed and merge in remembered tranquillity. Bishop Williams of Leicester, for example, remembered a game of sardines for Princess Anne and Prince Charles when he tried to squeeze into a nook behind the curtains already packed with royalty and was finally driven to the extremity of half-hiding beneath a knee-hole desk.

During his stay a fight between Princess Margaret's Sealyham and the royal corgis occurred in the drawing-room. One hopes that a visiting American bishop was similarly impressed by a valet-footman who even took woollen underpants away to be pressed, and other guests have been elated to find gold plate still used at dinner.

II

The Queen's great-grandfather could display his costly

improvements in the Sandringham gardens and jovially say "All Persimmon!" It has been the Queen's good fortune to have a racehorse of similar quality in the white-socked Aureole, descendant from the same St. Simon who sired Persimmon.

Unlike King Edward VII's horse, Aureole was only a Derby runner-up but his seven great races in the years 1952–54 proved him the finest horse in Europe and the victories of his progeny have placed him impeccably among the lasting influences of the Turf.

Retired to stud at Wolferton, his services averaged forty a year at six hundred guineas, a handsome contribution to Sandringham expenses. In his lush white-fenced meadow, with its reed-thatched shelter, Aureole in fact set the quietly elegant and prosperous tone of the royal estate. In the classic world of bloodstock, his stud fee was by no means expensive, although double that of his stud companion, Doutelle.

Grossing annually an average £37,700, the two stallions indirectly paid for the trimming of road verges and hedges, the servicing of the stable clock and the maintenance of woodland paths. They helped to pay the rates and met local incidentals such as the timely treatment of woodworm in the tower of Sandringham Church. The expenditure on fuel, gas, electricity and water when the Court was in residence, however, was charged to government funds under the Royal Palaces vote. The joint annual outgoing for Sandringham and Balmoral on this score alone was officially stated to be £3,792.

Some 50,000 people visit the Sandringham gardens each year but stud revenues presumably go a long way towards upkeep, and the garden receipts of about £3,000 entirely benefit charity under the National Gardens Scheme.

The show garden within its red-brick walls no longer clings to the opulent Edwardian style. The bold pergola and Alma-

Tadema benches have the slightly neglected cast-off air of similar fittings in every garden in the land. Around Humbert's deep-gabled and stylish mid-Victorian Gardener's Cottage the geometric beds of a Victorian parterre are permitted to remain, or have perhaps been deliberately restored, with their geraniums and heliotrope, lobelias and alyssum, creating a charming period picture that evinces the imaginative sensibilities of the owner.

Only the enthusiast need discover that the geraniums are of an improved strain, the sturdy Muriel Parsons variety from a seedling found by accident, named after the daughter of Mr. Harry Parsons, the head gardener, winning the Award of Merit of the Royal Horticultural Society and cross-bred and cultivated under Sandringham glass.

Probably the leading feature of present-day Sandringham is its progressive economy. The precept that the stately homes of England must now be self-supporting is nowhere better fulfilled. The unremitting commercial effort might, one thinks, have won the approval of astute King Edward VII, if not of King George V.

When the government closed their flax factory on the estate, the mill and warehouse sheds were converted into a bacon piggery of the Danish kind, with heated floors, automatic feeding, infra-red lamps in the sowing pens, and land and room for two thousand beasts. A flax store not wanted in this enterprise became a modern apple grading and packing station, with refrigerated storage for one hundred tons. There are fifty-seven acres of dessert apples and the wrappers, embodying a triangle and a circle with the words "Royal Fruit Farms, Sandringham, Norfolk" have become a familiar sight at Covent Garden and other markets.

On the farming side a radical policy change became evident in 1961 when the Queen replaced her herd of Red Polls, the milk cattle native to East Anglia, with a herd of Scottish Blue Greys for milk production. The grazing was moreover transferred from the marsh-flats, where the yield of wheat has proved twice the national average, to the hundreds of acres of reclaimed heath on the higher slopes where, behind sheltering rhododendrons, ploughing contractors had transformed the scene.

In all this, of course, one sees the vigorous hand of Prince Philip. Management, however conscientious, is stimulated by enterprising direction. The story is told of an official inspection to a quick-freezing plant where lunch with the chairman resolved into an offer to supply peas from Sandringham. Contracts were signed on an acreage basis for eighty acres. When the time came for renewal of contracts on a tonnage basis, difficulties in the negotiations were mentioned in the newspapers but it appears that Sandringham acumen won the day.

The sight of a carrot washing and grading machine at an agricultural show once made the Queen Mother pause and confide, "It would be a good thing. We have difficulties with carrots at Sandringham." The gypsy and caravan labour employed to pick the blackcurrant crop was similarly in the headlines when the Queen Mother visited the fields to talk, with her usual encouraging charm, to the pickers.

The royal picking rates averaging £21 per ton were thought to be good. The rates paid by processors of £200 per ton could show a pleasing return from twelve acres after clearing all growing costs.

The mushroom crop, too, is a Sandringham novelty now worthy of mention. There was a time when mushroom growers faced intensive questions whenever they met Prince Philip at agricultural shows or exhibitions. He clearly knew much of cultivation methods and the risks of diseases. An expert received parcels direct from the Prince enquiring, "what went wrong here, please?"

There are now twelve mushroom houses at Sandringham, the Sandringham baskets a familiar sight in Midland markets. In Birmingham, during a royal tour, the Queen and Prince Philip once happened to be shown some mushrooms by an elderly lady who had to confess that she did not know where they had come from. "You ought to be flogging some of ours," said Prince Philip cheerfully.

The Queen's innovations at Sandringham have followed a more traditional pattern. The retriever championships of the National Gun Dog League, for example, were held on one of the five estate farms in 1962 and the Queen followed the guns for most of the day, her enthusiasm sharpened by the entry of her own black Labrador, Sandringham Ranger.

Just as King George VI once noted, with a sense of incongruity, that he had spent four hours in a hide in a kale field, so his daughter spent five hours trudging through sugar beet, the waist-high plants sprayed from the air earlier in the summer, following the guns. Her own dog was disappointingly eliminated in the second round, though he showed himself to better advantage the following year.

The breeding and training of gun dogs has, in fact, become one of Her Majesty's enthusiasms, the kennels have been enlarged and fifteen black Labradors are kept "still in Queen Alexandra's kennels", as a handler explained, "with a new wing". For the first time in many years royal dogs have been placed on show in local Kennel Society contests.

Gun dogs were, indeed, a mutual enthusiasm of husband and wife. When Mrs. Grace Wheatley painted Prince Philip's portrait, she elected to depict him surrounded by all aspects and interests of his life, polo players, children at play to illustrate his interest in the National Playing Fields Association and so forth. "You've left one thing out," her sitter mentioned, and at his suggestion one of his favourite Sandringham gun dogs, a golden Labrador, was painted in prominently in the foreground.

It may be remarked that, happily, the Queen has not revived the Alexandrian idea of the dogs' cemetery. Those who wander in the grounds of Sandringham may nevertheless discover beneath an old yew — the symbol of immortality — a small inscribed stone commemorating "Susan, '44–'59. For about 15 years the faithful companion of the Queen". On either side of the mantelshelf in the main drawing-room, too, hang Miss Marjorie Porter's paintings of the royal Corgis, one of Susan, the other of her daughter, Sugar. Queen Alexandra, one thinks, would find a kindred touch in her great-granddaughter.

Curiously, the descendants of Queen Alexandra's pigeons — the Delmotte-Jurion strain — feature in the revival of royal patronage of pigeon-racing. The Queen's flight perhaps faced a crisis when an old gardener, Ernest Steele, retired, claiming sadly that no one else on the estate knew anything about the loft.

Eighty birds were however transferred to a loft near King's Lynn, where the Queen and Prince Philip made a point of visiting their new back-garden domain and the Queen's pigeons won seven races in 1963. The performance might have been still better, it was felt, but for the proximity of the Wash, and in 1964 the birds were released on training flights from shrimp boats to help cure their dislike of flying over water. The loft population shortly rose to 120, further races were won and a self-supporting trade in eggs and hatched birds began with fanciers.

III

The changes at Sandringham in the middle years of the twentieth-century have all veered, like the changes of the wider world, towards the incredible, the hitherto unimagined. Playing skittles with his cronies Albert Edward would have thought it inconceivable that seventy million people would one day peer into his bowling room. Yet this came to pass when the Queen made her first television Christmas broadcast in 1957, a new departure marking off the twenty-five years since her grandfather had first broadcast from General Knollys' room.

"It is inevitable that I should seem a rather remote figure to many of you," said the Queen. "But now at least for a few minutes I welcome you to the peace of my own home." It hardly mattered that the phrase was more sincere than literal. Apart from the ballroom, which was decked for Christmas, only the bowling alley in its dignified habit as the Long Library was large enough to receive the cameras and monitors, the batteries of lights and acoustic screens, and their control crews. Cables snaked everywhere over the floor, Prince Philip stood watching out of camera range, and the engineers thought it remarkable the Queen could seem composed and natural in the tense environment.

The broadcast was a pronounced success and a second sound and vision broadcast was made from Sandringham in 1958. Sitting at one end of a high-backed settee, the Queen could speak once more to the lonely. "We all need the kind of security that one gets from a happy and united family. Before I return to mine let me once again wish each one of you a very happy Christmas…" But the Queen was also aware that her broadcast inevitably separated thirty-five B.B.C. technicians from Christmas Day with their families, a factor that led to the making of a pre-recorded television message at Buckingham Palace in the year following. Though robbing the broadcast of some spontaneity, this was surely a decision that Mr. Motteux, that loneliest yet most gregarious of solitaries, would have applauded.

For his quiet ghost, too, no longer vexed by pew rents, time performs its miracle. The relay system of Sandringham Church echoes Christmas carols to the Sunday crowds, and Boy Scouts camp for a local jamboree in the trim park where he once admired his Marie Louise pears.

In her wildest imagination, that fashion-loving heiress, Mrs. Hoste Henley, could not have foreseen across the passage of two centuries that another heiress would walk through the stubble fields or that somewhere between a copse and the barley-stacking, a Queen would lose a wristlet watch given to her by the President of France. A unique platinum miniature, the watch was presented to the Queen when she was only twelve years old and worn in Westminster Abbey on her wedding day and although Army searchers with mine detectors, estate workers, Boy Scouts and Girl Guides searched for weeks, it was never found.

Once, long ago, a watch was lost before at Sandringham, after a day with the hunt when Henry Chaplin was leading the Princesses Maud and Victoria home across country and was unseated when his horse stumbled. Finding that his watch was missing, the trio returned to the spot the following day and there was the watch, deeply embedded in a furrow. But even the depth and pitch of the furrows have changed with modern farming machinery.

Such incidents would scarcely merit report, except at Sandringham. It is, after all, the home of the Sovereign, constantly subject to a blaze of publicity that would have seemed incandescent to the Cobbes of three hundred years ago. At the same time, it shares some of the privileges of the Crown as well as the disadvantages. The private estate of today comprises 20,000 acres, and their revenues have been held liable for tax, but since the estate of the Sovereign is exempt from death duties, Sandringham enjoys an advantage above all other estates of the realm. This alone may justify deeper interest. The long line of Becks worked with reticence and Captain Fellowes sustained and surpassed their discretion, but when his retirement through age in 1963–64 was announced, the gradual transfer to the new regime of Mr. Julian Lloyd was assessed in twelve inches in a national newspaper, a space never accorded before to a chartered profession.

One wonders whether the astute Becks took shares in the Norfolk Estuary Company when it began optimistically reclaiming the marshes of the Wash in the days of Spencer Cowper. Six hundred acres of saltings are being reclaimed today under Crown Estate auspices, and the future royal tenure of Sandringham seemed to receive a firm guarantee in 1964 when the Crown Estates Commissioners offered £223,500 for the Estuary shares, a figure so curiously close to the price that Albert Edward, the Prince of Wales, gave for his own first Sandringham purchase.

Now, as then, Sandringham is the home of an ordinary family placed in extraordinary circumstances, but the alleviations of privacy and simplicity are more sought after than of old. Instead of the tenants' ball the Queen pours tea at a Women's Institute meeting, sitting with the wives of the postmaster and an electrician and a retired estate watchman.

Instead of the County ball, the Queen presents school prizes — and in the ballroom there are sometimes amateur travel films and nature films made by the Queen herself. Homely paintwork fading in the sun and the rain, the scent of new-mown grass beneath the terrace, Sandringham changes even its pleasures in more simple patterns.

The year 1968 marked a century since a married couple with four children formed the family unit of the royal estate. After a hundred years, a Prince of Wales could still call Sandringham home. The substance of humankind is no less permanent than brick and mortar.

ABRIDGED BIBLIOGRAPHY

Apart from the acknowledgments given at the end of this book, and private information, the author's sources include the following:

History of Norfolk, Blomefield, 1805.
The Paston Letters.
Sandringham, Past and Present, Mrs. Herbert Jones, 1884.
Eighteen Years on the Sandringham Estate, The Lady Farmer, 1879.
Hunstanton and its Neighbourhood, P. Wilson and Geo. Webster. Editions, 1864–1903.
Norfolk Annals, Charles Mackie.
The King's Homeland, W. A. Dutt, 1904.
The Letters of Horace Walpole.
The Prince Consort and his Brother, Hector Bolitho.
Queen Victoria and Her Son, Sir George Arthur.
King Edward VII, Sir Sidney Lee.
King Edward VII, E. F. Benson.
King Edward VII As a Sportsman, A. E. T. Watson.
A Sailor's Life, Sir Henry Keppel.
Archbishop Magee, John MacDonnell.
The Letters of Disraeli to Lady Bradford & Lady Chesterfield.
Correspondence of Sarah Spencer, Lady Lyttelton.
The Letters of Lady Augusta Stanley, ed. Hector Bolitho.
My Memories, Lord Suffield.
Memoirs of Prince Christopher of Greece.
My Fifty Years, HRH Prince Nicholas of Greece.
The Letters of Tsar Nicholas and the Empress Marie.
Marlborough House and Its Occupants, Arthur H. Beavan.

The Private Life of Queen Alexandra, Hans Madol.
Queen Alexandra, Sir George Arthur.
What I Know, C. W. Stamper.
My First Sixty Years, Lady Maud Warrender.
Reminiscences of Sir Henry Irving, Bram Stoker.
Empty Chairs, Squire Bancroft.
Unpredictable Queen, E. E. P. Tisdall.
Samuel Wilberforce, His Diaries & Correspondence.
From My Private Diary, Daisy, Princess of Pless.
Memoirs, Sir Almeric Fitzroy.
Reminiscences, Lady Randolph Churchill.
Memoirs, Lord Fisher.
Journals & Letters, Lord Esher.
Four Studies in Loyalty, Christopher Sykes.
The Empress Frederick Writes to Sophie, ed. Arthur Gould Lee.
Cosmo Gordon Lang, J. G. Lockhart.
King George V, Harold Nicholson.
A King's Story, HRH The Duke of Windsor.
King's Nurse, Beggar's Nurse, Sister Catherine Black.
The King In His Country, Aubrey Buxton.
Fit For a King, F. J. Corbitt.
Fire Service Memories, Sir Aylmer Firebrace.
Royal Gardens, Lanning Roper.
Zeppelins over England, Kenneth Poolman.
Bishop's Wife — But Still Myself, Cicely Williams.
Crowded Life, Lady Cynthia Colville.
Grace and Favour, Loelia, Duchess of Westminster.
Not All Vanity, Baroness de Stoeckl.
Silver and Gold, Norman Hartnell.
Holkham Hall, James Laver.
English Architecture Since the Regency, H. S. Goodhart-Rendel.
The Buildings of England, NW & South Norfolk, Nikolaus

Pevsner.

The Annual Register, Dictionary of National Biography.

The Norfolk Handbook.

The East Anglia Handbook, etc. etc.

The Files of The Times, King's Lynn Advertiser, The Norfolk Gazette, Gardener's Chronicle, Illustrated London News, Country Life, Harper's Magazine, The Builder, The Architect, etc. etc.

ACKNOWLEDGEMENTS

Her Majesty The Queen enjoys the possession of several official residences in her public role as monarch. Buckingham Palace, Windsor Castle, St. James's Palace and the Palace of Holyroodhouse, Kensington Palace and Hampton Court are all State property of this kind, held in right of the Crown. Sandringham House is the Queen's only private home in England.

From the first plan to the first brick, this book thus commemorates the centenary of one of the best-known private country houses in the world. It has been my task and my privilege to chart a hundred years of royal domestic history and yet, apart from Mrs. Herbert Jones' early historical essay, which appeared in the eighties, and W. A. Dutt's account of the surrounding countryside, published in 1904, I have found myself in a curiously unexplored literary terrain.

At the outset I should like to thank the Royal Institute of British Architects for according me the facilities of their library. Others to whom I am indebted include the Earl of Leicester and his land agent, Mr. F. Sydney Turner, for information on Holkham Hall, and Mrs. P. Villiers-Stuart of Beachamwell Hall who so kindly overcame the disadvantages of her ninetieth year to give me her useful comments on the Motteux and Cowper families, based on knowledge handed down from her great-grandfather.

I am obliged to my neighbour, Lord Ponsonby of Shulbrede, for permission to quote from the letters of Henry Ponsonby, and to Mr. Hector Bolitho for allowing me to draw on the letters of Lady Augusta Stanley.

Mr. Harold A. Albert was again at my side for editorial collaboration.

I was indebted at all times to the helpful archivists and librarians of the Norfolk Record office, the City of Norwich Museum, the Norwich Central Library, the Carnegie Library of King's Lynn, the London Library, the Royal Horticultural Society, the Victoria and Albert Museum and the British Museum.

I must further express acknowledgment to the following publishers for kindly permitting quotation from copyright material: Messrs. John Murray for *The Letters of Queen Victoria* and *King George V, A Personal Memoir* by John Gore; Messrs. Allen and Unwin for *Queen Mary* by James Pope-Hennessy; Messrs. Macmillan for *King George VI* by Sir John Wheeler-Bennett and *Reminiscences* by Constance, Lady Battersea; Messrs. Eyre & Spottiswoode for *Recollections of Three Reigns* by Sir Henry Ponsonby; Messrs. Hodder and Stoughton for *A Norfolk Diary* by John Armstrong; Messrs. Longmans, Green for an extract from *Lord Palmerston* by Herbert C. Bell; Messrs. Collins for *Triumph in the West* by Sir Arthur Bryant; and Messrs. Hutchinson for *Embassies of Other Days* by Walburga, Lady Paget, *My Fifty Years* by H.R.H. Prince Nicholas of Greece, *Just a Little Bit of String* by Ellaline Terriss and *Thatched With Gold* by Mabell, Countess of Airlie. I must make it clear also that the copyright in the quotations from Queen Mary's Journals and Letters is reserved, as is the specific copyright in certain interior photographs of Sandringham House.

HELEN CATHCART

A NOTE TO THE READER

If you have enjoyed this book enough to leave a review on **Amazon** and **Goodreads**, then we would be truly grateful.
The Estate of Helen Cathcart

Sapere Books is an exciting new publisher of brilliant fiction and popular history.

To find out more about our latest releases and our monthly bargain books visit our website:
saperebooks.com

Printed in Great Britain
by Amazon